SHINE ON YOU CRAZY DAISY

VOLUME 1

COMPILED BY TRUDY SIMMONS

THE DAISY CHAIN GROUP PUBLISHING HOUSE

CONTENTS

Printed in the United Kingdom
First Printing, September 2021

ISBN: 9781739914806 (paperback)
ISBN: 9781739914813 (eBook)

The Daisy Chain Group International Ltd
Hampshire, UK
connect@thedaisychaingroup.com

Book Cover Design: Gemma Storey from Infinity Creative
Photo Credit of Trudy Simmons: Nisha Haq Photography

This book is dedicated to....

All the businesswomen that are showing up and putting themselves out there to be seen and heard. We are all in this together...this is for you to take inspiration, that we are all on a similar journey, but taking different paths, with varying bumps along the way to here.

You can do it! Keep going!

ACKNOWLEDGMENTS

This is to acknowledge and appreciate all of those that have contributed and shared a piece of their journey with us all in this book. Thank you for your courage and tenacity. You are all inspirational.

I would like to thank my sister Jody and acknowledge that those who aren't with us can be our biggest inspirations. Never far from my mind. Everyone has the potential to shape and change someone's day for the better, that was (and is) who Jody was for me.

There is no "way-man" that I would have come up with the idea for this book without you. Your unwavering support and gentle encouragement is all new to me and I am grateful.

To the Facebook communities that I run - Hampshire Women's Business Group and International Women's Business Group for showing me each and every day that whatever we are going through, we are all there for each other. For being the communities that we all call "our lounge-room" where we come to share, ask for help, support, advice and give from our expertise without expectations. Community is everything on this lonely road. Come and join ours, it is the best - tee hee!

INTRODUCTION

This book is about creating a platform for businesswomen to have an inspirational voice and to share their stories with others, to show that this entrepreneurial rollercoaster is the highs AND the lows and that we navigate them all differently, but hopefully with a tribe/team of people that support our vision to our success – whatever that looks like, and it is different for everyone.

The stories were written in July 2021 - 16 months after Covid has hit our countries, our families and our businesses. Things are still raw, but the resilience is there!

Each story is unique, each story is REAL, each story offers a piece of insight, motivation and encouragement when we need it the most.

These are un-edited chapters of real stories from women that have been where you are and have stories to share about how to find your way, not feel isolated, find out what you can do, rather than feeling stuck in what you think you can't do.

Here…. Are their stories!! Bong bong…

Charity donation

As we gain, so can we give – that is my philosophy of running my own business. 10% of the profits from this book will be donated to the bereaved families of the NHS who have died while looking after us and our families during the Corona-Virus pandemic.

To find out more, or to donate, please visit this website – https://gofund.me/8aed0fc3

1

THE WAY OF THE CRAZY DAISY

Trudy Simmons

There are things that we are "told" as children; or things that we are taught through our lives that affect how we show up in the world. I spent years hearing all these messages and feeling like I couldn't run my own business for the fears of going against these ingrained stories – and then … when I started my own business, it took years to un-learn these stories to help me to be visible in a noisy market.

See if any of these resonate with you:

· Be a good girl
· You're too much
· You're not enough
· You don't know enough
· Do as you're told
· Don't make too much noise
· Don't be the centre of attention
· Don't be too happy (yes, I have been told this)

- Just blend in
- This is what is expected of you
- This is where you will get to
- This is what you will do for a job
- These are your options
- Don't make waves
- Your ideas make you look stupid
- Don't do it – you'll fail
- You can't do that
- You're too out-there
- You're a drama queen
- You're too aggressive
- Stop being bossy
- That's a crazy idea

I spent my whole life thinking I was too dramatic (excuse me – faints in mock disgust). When actually, when I came to the un-learning, I then relearnt *who I am* and what I want to be known for.

And this is where the gold-dust is. What is your unique-crazy? What is your USP (unique selling point)? Who are you when you are not being told who you can be, or who you should be? (*Starts blowing raspberries loudly at all the people telling what is right for me.)

Burnout

I went through years of a brilliant career, loving everything I was doing and how I showed up – until – I was being told who I was allowed to be in the business. And this has happened a lot!

The expectations of getting suited-n-booted (high heeled!), the expectations of being quiet in meetings unless spoken too (as if!), the expectations of not being able to have an opinion because it was viewed as aggressive or confrontational (pfft!). All of this and the years of swallowing what I thought, who I was and how I showed up, led to massive burnout.

After I stopped my corporate career, I took a year out. Because I had to. I was dead inside.

I didn't know how to be in the world without someone telling me who to be. I didn't know how to be around people without allowing them to dictate how I was allowed to act. Don't get me wrong; it was all my own doing. I was a born people pleaser. But at the age of 35 (spring chicken!!), I had to find myself; I had to get back to how to be happy; I had to work out how to create my own life *and* my own business. Scared? Ummm ... poopy-pants-a-rama!!

Finding my people

I was lucky. I very quickly found a group of local entrepreneurial women and soon realised that they liked me for me. I realised that I had a voice, that I could contribute and that I was really, really good at creating an environment where other businesswomen could be themselves, show up, turn up and be seen and heard.

Within months of starting my own business coaching business, I created networking events so we could get together, share our businesses, share our ideas and support each other. I was hearing things being said about me that were complimentary (thank goodness!) and started to build my confidence that I was enough.

I had been through years of bullying, being talked down to, being told that I was *too much*, being asked to be quiet because I was too happy (what the actual!!) and now ... I was going to build a brand and a business on all of the things that I was told were against me.

. . .

3

COMPILED BY TRUDY SIMMONS

Where to begin?

Well, I said I was lucky..., but that's a dumb word. I wasn't lucky at all. My darling sister Jody died, and it shook me to my core, it took all that I had been and made me start again. I had no idea who I was. I lost a part of my identity. I lost the ability to be who people needed me to be and I was only able to be... me. I dropped every mask that I had been taught to wear – trained to wear. I didn't have the capacity or the strength to "pretend" to be someone else. And I started from there.

Firstly, grief is a very individual process, and I was very much alone in my grief. I had never known anyone who died before, and I didn't know how I was "supposed" to act. (Act being a very apt word...).

My grief meant that I had a massive opportunity to be vulnerable – which I had never allowed myself to be before. It gave me courage to show up in little ways, rather than feeling like I had to be the life-of-the-party. It helped me to get to know the people around me on another level. It gave me the strength to not show up when I didn't want to – I used to show up because I had to.

I saw that people that weren't used to me being me, or hadn't seen this quieter side of me, dropped away. I saw that the people who needed me to give them my energy left, and that was needed; I didn't have extra energy to share. I saw that the friends who wanted me to be their crutch weren't there for me in my time of need.

Know, like and trust

Having your own business is a brilliant leveller. You will find that the circle of people you trust changes and becomes closer. Some people who have been around you for years will fall away because they don't understand that "working from home" means you work harder and might not have the time or the energy to drop everything when they need you (especially when it isn't reciprocated!).

What I have learnt, seen, and taught is that when you have your own business, you need to grow the "know, like and trust" factor with your audience, your business friends and your clients/customers.

When I was in a state of grief, when I was trying to find who I was after that, I went back to the basics. What do I want to be known for? How can I engage with people so they can get to know me for that? How can I show up so they can like me? Who am I when I like myself? How can I build trust? What does trust look like for me with the people around me now?

Asking these questions and implementing them in how I show up has built my business from a very solid foundation and built engaged communities of businesswomen who want to be more visible in safe environments.

Here is my formula for success – BAHAHAHA! If there was one, having your own business would be a breeze, but we are all on the rollercoaster, riding the highs (which are so high!) and the lows (which are back-breaking and soul destroying at times).

What I have witnessed, encouraged, and fostered in anyone who comes along to my networking events is: to build your confidence in being visible, you need to take 5 seconds of courage and show up to networking. When we connect and engage with other people as we are, we find our tribe of people to be around and encourage us. When we feel encouraged and motivated, we are happier. When we are happier, we build our confidence, and when we build our confidence we are more able to be visible. And we all need to be visible to build our audience, our potential customers, and our businesses.

From the very first networking event I attended, I knew I had found a group of people who 'got it'. They get the ups and downs, they get the "working from home", they get the 'juggling act', they get the 'wearing fifteen hats at once', they get the 'over-whelm', they get the down days...the good days... the produc-tive days...the couch days... they get it all – and it is why networking has become such an important part of my week and my business.

Joy and authentic connection

It gives me so much joy to see the beautiful bunch of busi-nesswomen who turn up as themselves and share their stories – many of which are in this book. To see someone who might be struggling at the beginning of the meeting, who leaves with a smile on their face and a spring in their step. The person who is celebrating a win but isn't sure if they can "brag" about what they have achieved – celebrate it all; we want to hear all about it. The person who is stuck and then meets someone else who can help them. The person who knows someone else who needs an attendee's services – and so word spreads. I have people from my communities saying they can get 60% of their business from attending our networking events, by growing and nurturing that "know, like and trust". Networking has changed. It is no longer about turning up, passing out business cards (I haven't owned business cards in over 5 years!), talking at people and then leaving. Now, we-is-CRAZY! We have fun, we laugh, we engage, we show our personalities so people can buy from people. We tell our stories, we share our businesses, we talk about what we do and how we help our clients, and we engage in what others are doing, how others are doing, how we can help the people in that room. Virtual hugs are a must. Support is a part of the makeup of the meetings.

Being a Crazy Daisy means you have been brave enough to show who you are, what you want to do, and you have put yourself out there to do it. We want to meet you and celebrate that with you. Whether you are making hair slides, creating graphics, running an accountancy practice, designing websites or teaching people how to market themselves effectively – we all need help and support, and networking is the way that I have found that makes me forget that list of things at the beginning of this chapter; all the things that I was told would affect how I showed up. Now I am me. I am a Crazy Daisy, and I love my business – it makes me happy!

BIO

Trudy Simmons is a Clarity and Productivity Business Coach for women entrepreneurs, with a truckload of empathy and a little bit of hard-arse!

She helps you find out what you want to do, why you want to do it, and how to get it done!

She loves to show her audience how to become more successful by getting clarity, taking action and following through. Trudy helps people move from being stuck and not knowing the next step, to getting their shizzle done. She knows what keeps you up at night – the thousand ideas that are germinating in your brain – and she knows how to sort them into "no go", "maybe later", and "hells yes", and get done what is really important to your success.

She is the creator and founder of: The Crazy Daisy Networking Events, The Accountability Club, The Spectacular Online Business Symposium, The Spectacular Challenge to £1 Million, and The Happy Business Mastermind.

The Daisy Chain Group – www.thedaisychaingroup.com

2

A REBEL WITH AN EMERGING CAUSE

Gillian Jones-Williams

I wasn't supposed to succeed. No one thought I would make anything of myself, and everyone thought I was going to waste my life. Because at age 16, the signs were not looking good. My mother had a chronic Bi-polar condition, so I had a very turbulent childhood. Ironically, the benefit of having a disturbed home life is that it gives you an excuse to rebel, and I certainly was not the most impressive student at school. There was no doubt that I had the capability, but my behaviour and lack of attendance led the school to pretty much write me off. Having said that, I miraculously did manage to walk away with a fairly respectable clutch of exam results, enough to get me into college, but after 2 weeks I decided I needed to leave home, which meant getting a job so I dropped out of college. In a last-ditch attempt to help me get a job my father sent me to a secretarial college where I found I had an extraordinary skill for touch typing – which has stood me in great stead over the years as I eventually also became an author and have now published three books. But what I didn't know is that I would later spend most of my time supporting women to overcome their own fears and become the best that they could be.

It wasn't easy to find my career path but after a series of bar work and secretarial jobs, I finally found a job I liked doing and was good at – it basically involved being good at talking, which for me, was no problem at all! The job was as a recruitment consultant, and this became my career. I loved interviewing people and persuading clients to employ them, and I excelled in this, hitting commission after commission. I was even promoted to a Regional Franchise Manager where I travelled the country training others to do the job. I ended up working in a recruitment agency where I was number two to the managing director.

One day, one of our clients asked if we did customer service training and of course I said 'yes'. I didn't know much about training but we trained all our internal staff so I figured it couldn't be that difficult! They wanted all six hundred of their staff trained so we put in a bid and won the contract. I designed and delivered the first day's training, and the clients were really happy. The next day I was in the agency offices and there was a case of sexual harassment between one of the male consultants, (who had been drinking at lunchtime) and the part-time receptionist. As the MD was on holiday, I dealt with it and interviewed the consultant. He had sobered up and was very embarrassed and said that the best thing for him to do was to resign and I agreed. However, he was a big earner and when the MD returned from holiday, he decided that the situation was not that serious and asked the man to return, even offering him more money. I was deeply disturbed by this and said I couldn't work for an organisation that condoned sexual harassment. I was told that, if I was choosing to leave, it would be immediate.

I was marched to my desk to clear out my possessions and escorted from the premises.

The next morning at home, I had a call from the client who had booked the customer service training. I told them that I didn't work for the agency anymore, but they said that they had bought 'me'. They then said "I guess you are now unemployed" which I hadn't really thought much about but had to agree I was, and so they said they wanted me to deliver the training and so would contract with me directly. So, there it was, I had six hundred people to train, no company name, no idea of how to invoice and no experience of running my company. And within a week I had a lawsuit from the agency for Breach of Contract! It would have been extremely easy to give up there and then and think that being a business owner wasn't for me – it was easy to get jobs in those days and I could have just gone and worked for a big corporate organisation, but I fought the lawsuit, won and continued the training.

That was 25 years ago and the company, Emerge Development Consultancy was born, despite my children (a son and a daughter) being incredibly young and my lack of experience in owning a business. It was hard, I was running my business from a tiny office at home, with a mini photocopier to print handouts. There was no internet, so designing courses took many hours of research and visits to the library to find books. In those days there was no social media, and the business was built on referrals – I would work hard to build relationships with my client contact and every time they moved to another company, they would take us with them. Within 7 years we had started to turn over in excess of a million pounds and were working with some huge corporate clients. We were renowned for our expertise in leadership development, organisational change, and women's development. An irony for me as I was often the least educated person in the room, with a chronic self-esteem issue caused by my mother during childhood.

There were many lessons I learnt in my career and here are a couple of important ones. In the early years I had two partners which didn't work out before I had a successful business partnership lasting almost 20 years. I learnt a lot from that – when you are new to running your own business, it is easy to be distracted by people who look as if they bring a lot to the table and make promises that give you confidence. Running a business is lonely so you may imagine that having a partner will make it easier, but only if it is the right partner. So, my first tip would be that if you are thinking of going into partnership with someone, do a lot of work up front on values, working styles, vision, and boundaries. It is quite easy to set up a partnership but extracting yourself is far more complicated.

And I have learnt the power of tenacity – sometimes things get really tough, and it is so easy to think about just getting a job in a supermarket stacking shelves, but I learnt that in those times you need to take a breath, remind yourself of your higher purpose and get creative.

Never more so than in the last 18 months.

As 2020 dawned, my 60th year, everything had come together for the business, the order book was looking full, the team were working well, we were taking on a new person on the 1 April and to top it all I had been nominated as one of the top 100 UK Female Entrepreneurs in the F; Entrepreneur #Ialso campaign.

As I left for my annual skiing holiday at the beginning of March, talk of the pandemic was circulating and during that week, as Italy locked down, I started to watch my business disappear. Every booking was cancelled, and we were suddenly left staring at an empty order book. We had only delivered our training and coaching face-to-face, and we had no idea how to deliver virtually – plus our clients were all waiting to see how long the lockdown lasted so we started to lose money hand over fist. Our overheads were enormous, and our income was virtually nothing. It was decision time – if I closed the business down fast, I could retain the reserves that I had in the company and I could still get work as an independent associate. But I had put too much work into this business to have it decimated by a virus – and I had an amazing team who had been with me for between 10 and 20 years. So, I took the decision to keep it going, but, on the condition, we had to be breaking even by September 2020.

We agreed that as we had lost everything, we were now a start-up and we had to start behaving like a start-up, creating new products and services, aggressive marketing, keeping our clients not just warm but 'red hot' by supporting them through their problems, and never entertaining failure. We focussed on every small win – from previously winning bids worth £100k we celebrated every £1000 we made, learnt everything we could about making virtual training exciting, persuaded our clients that online courses would be equally effective and worked 14-hour days from home every day of the week. It worked, and in September 2020 we started to break even.

At the time of writing this in July 2021 we are happily in profit again with a healthy pipeline, a steady flow of opportunities and ambitious growth plans. And as I genuinely believe in the power of paying things forward, I published a book about the experience, a daily diary of events of the first 3 months of the pandemic and my struggle to save the business called "Locked Down but Not Out" which went on to Amazon in January to raise money for the bereaved families of NHS workers. I am so glad that I did it as I was concerned we would forget the sacrifices that these people made, and it needed to be recorded.

We learnt so much through that year, the need for courage and tenacity, the importance of communication, how crucial it was to look after our clients and how, if we pushed the boundaries of innovation and trusted our gut, we could produce amazing ideas and products. It also taught me not to give up on things too early, to trust in the process and always believe in myself.

Going forward I plan to continue to grow the business, to develop women internationally with our RISE Empowering Women's Programme, to help them learn that, no matter where you come from or whether people believe in you, you can always succeed if you believe that you can. I also want to hang on to the lessons that I learnt during the pandemic, both professionally and personally to make every minute of my life count.

BIO

Gillian Jones-William is Managing Director of Emerge Development Consultancy. Emerge is internationally renowned for unlocking potential that achieves transformation within organisations by providing a full range of bespoke development and coaching solutions. We are proud to be working with leading organisations in the UK and globally. Gillian founded the RISE Women's Development Programme which is delivered both in the UK and Middle East. She is also the co-author of How to Create a Coaching Culture, 50 Top Tools for Coaching and the author of Locked Down but Not Out.

Emerge Development Consultancy – www.emergeuk.com

3

IN MY OWN TIME

Bev Fowler

My story starts back in 2010. I was a mum of two little boys working as a children's nanny, taking my little ones along with me. It was hard work, exhausting and lots of fun. However, juggling family and work life was certainly an art, and from experience I knew that my little ones would grow up at an alarming speed and I didn't want to miss a thing.

Many a daydream was had, as I contemplated the future. I wanted to start something new, to be my own boss and work entirely at my own speed. How could I achieve all this while raising my family? And still be there for the nursery and school runs and after-school mayhem all while making a living, and without the need for childcare.

The first struggle I had to overcome was my own hang ups about being dyslexic. A huge barrier had built up over the years. I felt that it had held me back at school and had a huge impact on my career choices. But here I was, wanting more for my future and wanting even more to show my young boys that if you really desire something and you put in the work, then you can be anything you want to be in life. I wanted to be a strong role model to them, with a good work ethic.

Playing to my strengths

Being a very practical, hands-on person, the obvious career choice would be one playing to my strengths. I stumbled upon keepsake jewellery and an opportunity to buy into a franchise. All training and business back up was included! However, it just didn't sit right with me. It would never truly be my business; there would be restraints on what and how I could sell and what I could make. I was disappointed but didn't let that stop me.

With lots more research and some encouragement from another mum in business, I found a training course that interested me and would get me heading in the right direction. I knew straight away that this was the right move forward.

I'm creative and love to make things that bring others joy. And so keepsake jewellery was the perfect fit, and Treasure Box was born. Making jewellery with such sentiment makes my heart sing. I have always been a keen learner and have spent hours pushing myself to learn new skills online and attend jewellery courses from time to time.

Of course friends and family were my first customers. Then very soon it became their friends and then their friends, until my name was out there, and I was getting recommendations far beyond a trackable link.

While attending a village show with my jewellery early on in my journey, I was approached by a local boutique who wanted to sell my jewellery in their shop! Wow, just wow! I was so flattered and excited and of course said yes! It was one of my best decisions. The owner and her staff were also mums in business and were so supportive and inspiring.

I always had in mind that I was going to build my business at my own speed. Keeping it small enough that I could keep my family at the heart of everything. I was in it for the long game. At times this was really hard. Keeping the pot simmering when I wanted it to boil! Sometimes I would get frustrated by onlookers who would ask questions like "how's your little hobby going?" or "so how much do you earn from your little business?" I could feel my defences go up. I felt like they didn't see this as a business or that I could make a real 'go' of it! As far as I was concerned it was moving along at exactly the right speed. I was not going to let their lack of faith get me down, in fact all it did was spur me on.

Growth and outsourcing

My workspace was a tiny desk in our spare room, so I had to be very organised to keep on top of orders. I dreamt of having a website, but it was such a big block for me. I just had no idea where to even start, as tech is not my forte! I asked a local website designer to help me, and she was amazing and very patient. This was my biggest outsourcing so far, and it felt a little overwhelming. It was hard to put my ideas across to another person. I had far too many ideas and jewellery pieces that I wanted to include. It was a great website, but I lacked the skills to keep it up to date and so very soon it felt dated, complicated and missing my personality. I gave it no love or attention, but it was built and that was the main thing.

My top supporters have always been my closest friends and family. They believed in me from the start and cheered me on from the side-lines. Shamelessly plugging my jewellery to anyone who would listen (and even those who weren't listening). I began to grow steadily as the years passed, mostly through local craft shows, selling in the boutique, through word of mouth and the occasional online sale, and upgraded my workspace to a little studio.

Digging deeper

Jump forward to 2019. Both our boys now at secondary school, it was time to dig deep and grow. But how was I going to do that? I had waited so long for the time to be right. Now I was just a little stuck.

Having felt that it was such a lonely world out there for a one woman business. I was often feeling inadequate, unsupported, always comparing myself to others, sometimes floundering and not sure how to move forwards. I felt that I was missing the skills and confidence to push myself forwards. I needed more business support and wanted to surround myself with like-minded businesswomen.

While scrolling on Facebook I found two amazing groups, Hampshire Women's Business Group and Jewellers Academy. I was totally inspired. How had I missed this resource? It was brimming with support. I could ask questions and not feel embarrassed or out of my depth. I had struck pure gold!

Then bam ... lockdown, a global pandemic! What now? No customers coming into my studio to buy jewellery, shops shut, everyone confined to their homes. Time to panic or time to dig even deeper!

I was so grateful to still be able to work, as my studio was in walking distance, and I worked alone. I had lots of stock silver to work with and the postal system was still up and running. There was a glimmer of hope on the horizon. But my online presence was in no way up to scratch! Luckily, I had signed up to an 8-week business bootcamp for jewellers – what better time than now to put all my efforts into a massive revamp?

I learnt I needed to identify who my ideal customer actually was and aim my social media posts to reach them. Pressure selling has never been my style, so I had a lot to learn about directing sales to my website in a more natural way. Guiding potential customers in the right direction to invest in my products. Updating my branding colours followed by lots of photography, and then a complete overhaul of my website. I needed to be online properly and fast! I'm not going to lie … it was hard work. Thank goodness for computer savvy teenage boys! They were so supportive and helped when I felt totally out of my depth.

Energised by all my hard work, I was so proud of myself. I re-listed all of my items on the website. Streamlining the customer's experience, updating all the products and making it look enticing. It paid off, and I started getting lots of online sales. Posting jewellery orders all around the country. I was using Facebook and Instagram to communicate with my ideal customers, which started getting my jewellery noticed more and more.

In turn, I have been able to share my experiences and knowledge with other small business owners. Encouraging them to follow their dreams and have faith in their own abilities – to be courageous and reach for the stars. Over the past year, I have had some lovely feedback from people saying that they find my social media posts are inspiring. I had no idea that my posting had had this effect on my followers. How could someone who was so afraid to put themselves out there have a positive impact?

Seeing how my jewellery impacts my customers is a massive drive to carry on. I get to make such personal and unique items. Some are made in celebration, others to mark a milestone, or made to hold a memory and for all sorts of other occasions, and my heart and soul are invested in each and every piece that leaves my studio.

So what do I want for my future? I want to grow Treasure Box, even bigger and even better, while surrounding myself with all the right people. I want to keep pushing myself forwards, building my confidence and continuing to develop my jewellery and business skills. I have the confidence in myself to make this happen and I am up for the challenge!

A word of advice

My advice to independent business owners is to never be afraid to ask for help and support. Follow your own plan and pathways and not someone else's. Believe and be confident in yourself. Take time out when you need to, you are the essence of your business, and no one wants a burn out!

When you are itching to get to work on a Monday morning, you know you are doing what you were born to do. Being creative in my jewellery business is what brings me so much joy.

BIO

Bev Fowler is a jewellery designer / maker and the face behind Treasure Box. She creates handcrafted silver keepsakes by impressing fingerprints, hand, foot and paw prints into silver. Alongside these modern day heirlooms, she also designs and makes collections of silver jewellery perfect to wear every day. She has lived in the beautiful county of Hampshire, England for all 42 years of her life.

Treasure Box – www.treasurebox.uk.com

4

ALL BECAUSE SHE SAID YES

Vie Portland

I am virtually unemployable.

I'm a middle aged woman with several disabilities who needs flexibility over the number of hours worked and where they are worked; and I need flexibility and understanding for the days I can't work at all. Not exactly an ideal candidate for an employer.

For a few years, I thought my life was going to be a consistent hum of pain, depression, and benefits; struggling for happiness and money; never feeling, or being, valued, because I didn't know what I was capable of. I had been told my physical and mental health would mean I would never work again. What was the point of me?

I truly hit the depths of despair.

Then, when things couldn't get any worse, I realised I was the only one who could change things. That was a terrifying prospect! What on earth could I do to change things?! I felt useless.

But, then I decided to start saying "yes" to things. I had been at my lowest and I knew the only way was up or, well, out. Surely anything had to be an improvement?

The first thing I said yes to was burlesque classes. I had always loved to dance, though was never encouraged to do it, so this was a big thing! I had no confidence and no self-belief, so I was incredibly worried I would be utterly rubbish!

But I wasn't! I was actually good! That was a surprise.

One of the other women in the class asked me to help her organise a show; I liked to feel useful, so I agreed. Then she said I would have to perform! Hell no!! I couldn't even cope with people singing "Happy Birthday" to me! I was usually the narrator in school plays so I could stand off to the side of the stage and only be seen and heard by the people performing. Performing on a stage, on my own, ridiculous!

But, she was incredibly persuasive.

I agreed to perform once, and once only. And I prepared to fail miserably and make an utter fool of myself. I would reassure myself that, when everything went completely wrong, I would move to a nunnery in the Himalayas; it seemed the only logical thing to do.

Completely surprisingly, the audience really liked me!

And, what was even more surprising, I went on to become an international performer. Me!! People booked me to perform not only all over the UK but in other places too! Bizarre!

People started saying that they really liked what I did, and that they would like me to teach them. Me? Teach? Baffling!

Around the same time, I had started wearing clothes that I had always dreamt of wearing: 1950s reproduction. I had been teaching myself how to feel good about myself, using my academic experience in psychology and counselling, and talking to myself more kindly, as I had done to all the children I had looked after in my previous careers; so I was feeling happy in myself and I felt confident enough to wear clothes I had previously felt only particular people could wear.

I had also started going to vintage events. I loved the opportunity to dance at them. And, again, people said they really liked how I danced, and they would ask me to teach them.

I decided to give it a go, and, within a couple of weeks, I taught my first burlesque workshop and my first dance workshop. People said I was a natural teacher. I was asked for more. That was nine years ago.

From dancing teacher to CIC

People began to comment on how the attendees of my classes had grown in confidence. They asked me to teach them how to feel good about themselves, but they didn't want to dance, and they certainly weren't taking their clothes off! So I started teaching body confidence workshops. Well, I called them body confidence workshops but, really, they covered several areas where confidence affects us.

A little later, I started to run a branch of a voluntary project that wanted to help eradicate period poverty in schools. The teaching staff would ask what I did, and I would tell them about the confidence workshops. They all said that it was really needed in their school.

I began to research how I could run confidence workshops in schools. I knew that many schools couldn't afford to pay for external facilitators to go in, so I wanted to find a way to make it work.

I found out about Community Interest Companies (CIC). As a CIC, you can apply for some grants and fundraise, and there isn't as much red tape; this sounded like the ideal solution!

In June 2019, VieNess Discover You Love You CIC was born.

Within a few days, it was awarded its first grant; within four months, it had received its first awards! I started making contact with schools, arranging workshops. I got booked for youth groups.

The CIC was gaining interest and momentum. It was very exciting!

A creative response to the pandemic

Then the pandemic arrived. All of my work was in person and, not being all that technically adept, I was very concerned about what I was going to do; I wasn't sure I could move online.

But, I knew I wanted to do something.

I love children's books! I have always loved to read them, and I feel they are a great way for everyone to learn, children and adults alike. With my CIC, I began to look for books that were about the things I taught about: acceptance, confidence, kindness. I have a wonderful collection.

I decided to use them.

I began to run story time sessions via Zoom. I would read a book linked to my work, then the children and I would have wonderful conversations around it, and I would set an activity. I really loved the sessions! Unfortunately, they brought very little money into the CIC so I realised I had to put my focus elsewhere.

Not long before the pandemic, I met the brilliant Dr. Jennifer Jones, a writing coach; she suggested I write a book to establish my expertise in my field. I had loved writing stories at school, and I enjoyed the writing classes I went to when my health first got worse, but I hadn't written properly in a long time. Jennifer, though, through her workshops, revived my creativity. I started thinking about other things I could do.

I began creating decks of cards. Self-help books are great, but sometimes, when you're really struggling with something, they can feel too big. I wanted my cards to be a "one step at a time" approach. The first two decks were A Little Box Full of Confidence and A Little Box Full of Happiness. I'm currently working on A Little Box Full of Family Fun, which is full of activities to help families talk more.

As I was working on the cards, the two lines I had had in my head for years for a children's book suddenly got bigger. I wrote a children's book!

The story is one to encourage imagination in both children and adults; I work with a lot of children who live in poverty and, frequently, they believe they can only do what their parents did. Sometimes, that would mean getting pregnant to get a council flat. I believe that if we're encouraged to dream big, we can achieve big things. I want children to read my book and create their own dreams to live up to.

It was also important to me, as a person with disabilities, to have the main character have a visible difference. But I didn't want their disability to be the point of the story; awareness raising stories are incredibly important but, for me, they also highlight our differences. I wanted my story to demonstrate that we all have far more in common than what separates us. Before we are anything else, before we are any label, we are all human first.

That book, *Where Are We Going?*, illustrated by the very talented Donna Mcghie, was self-published, via a crowdfunding campaign, in March 2021.

As I write this, I'm also working on my second children's book, *Who Am I?*, and a book for adults (that one doesn't have a title yet!), the book that Jennifer first approached me about. This book is part autobiographical and part guidance on how to find confidence and happiness. I'm hoping people will read it and realise that we are all far more capable than the limitations we, or others, put on ourselves. The children's book is another story featuring Emily, the little girl in the first book; in this one,

I aim to encourage conversations about all the wonderful things we are.

This is all incredibly wonderful but there have been some lows; there have been many months when money didn't come into my CIC; there have been times when I have doubted if I was doing the right thing. There have been so many times when I was exhausted from constantly showing up and schmoozing with people. But these things are part of running a business.

Now, well, what does the future hold? ANYTHING IS POSSIBLE!

Where am I going?

Fourteen years ago, I was at the lowest point a person could get to, and I truly believed I was worthless, incapable of anything. In the intervening years, I have had experiences that I thought "someone like me" could never have. I have gone from self-loathing to self-loving. I have worked with hundreds of women, teaching them to dance and how to be more confident. I've worked with hundreds of children and young people, helping them see what their strengths are, how incredible they are, and that we are all far more worthy than the number on the scales or the clothes size we wear.

I have made a difference.

For someone who thought they were incapable of changing anything, that's a pretty big deal.

Fourteen years ago, the thought of performing would have been utterly ridiculous. But I did it.

Ten years ago, I would never have thought I could be a teacher. But I did it.

Five years ago, I never would have thought people would come to me, asking me to teach them how to feel confident. But I did it.

Three years ago, I never thought I would be the founder of a

CIC and be talking at international events about my work. But I did it.

A year ago, I never thought I would be an author. But I am now.

All because I started saying "yes".

What can you say "yes" to?

BIO

Vie Portland is founder of VieNess Discover You Love You CIC, a Community Interest Company that teaches self-esteem and confidence to children, young people and vulnerable women. She coaches women one to one, to help them find their fabulous. She's a creator of happiness products. And she is an author of books for adults and children. She's very glad she said "yes".

Discover You Love You CIC – www.vieness.co.uk

5

PLAN TAKES SUDDEN DIVERSION

Liz Ranger

Have you ever been on a road trip? Your route is planned, and your destination known but during the journey you hit a diversion! Sometimes the diversion is planned with helpful signs that you trust and other times you are left to your own instincts.

Of course, 'Sat Navs' have helped with this dilemma, but I was not so lucky in life to have an immediate Sat Nav when my life took a sudden diversion.

Let's go back a few years and at age three I was inspired to care for others through a comic where Nurse Nancy cared for her toys. Move the clock forward to age eighteen and I fulfilled my dream and passion and trained to be a Children's Nurse in London. Caring and supporting children to get well and seeing their journey to health was a phenomenal privilege for me. My career took me over many parts of the south coast of England,

and it involved working with the Department of Health and speaking at national forums.

In 2016, however, my thirty-four-year nursing career came to a sudden end as I developed Post-Traumatic Stress Disorder (PTSD) and overnight I lost my identity, many colleague friends and my purpose and passion. This was certainly an unexpected change and at this point I was not being diverted but stuck and feeling unexpectedly lost.

PTSD is an anxiety disorder caused by very stressful, frightening or distressing events. Disturbing thoughts and feelings related to the event can be experienced long after the traumatic event. The event can be relived through flashbacks and there is a myriad of feelings and emotions which can be experienced.

PTSD is often aligned to the military and consequences of a war environment they have been exposed to. Yet having attended support groups I have seen there are many circumstances that can lead to PTSD. I personally have complex PTSD which means it was more than one event that led to my condition.

PTSD impacts a person through triggers related to the event which caused the PTSD. It is like opening a cupboard door and something falling out when you least expect it. The triggers can have a mental but also physical impact. Having these symptoms repeatedly happening led me to stay at home and isolate myself, as I felt safer and more in control. Though I may have felt safer this did not really help with my recovery or finding that diversion.

My diversion started through accessing many types of therapy and if I am honest, I really hated it. It was not the therapist that I hated but where I was on my journey. I needed to talk about things that triggered me. I tried medications but they had side effects that added to the horrible symptoms. Recovering from PTSD is a journey and revisiting therapy after periods of consolidation was key for me.

One thing that helped me find my diversion was having a small network marketing business. It provided me with some necessary plans and structures to start taking those first steps. I started meeting with people and offering a solution to people around their home finances. I realised that the feelings that I had experienced in nursing, of caring and appreciating others, could be found in other careers too. The PTSD did not need to define me.

I realised through different choices and business opportunities that came along I could be stronger and happier. The road trip was back in place! It was different to what I had imagined at age eighteen, but it was new and exciting.

During the 2020 pandemic, life was stalled again, as I am sure that it was for many. My business model could not be followed so another redirection was needed. These changes and re-directions require a growth mindset. I realised that I had been growing even when I had felt so challenged by the PTSD. I had moved from a fixed mindset that I could not do things to a mixed mindset (as small steps started) and then into the growth mindset.

So, during 2020 I was introduced to Passionate Marketing and completed a passion test with my mentor. Aligning your life and business to what you are passionate about makes you happier and fulfilled. As a nurse I had been passionate about caring for people, so they felt valued and appreciated. The passion test showed me I could do that in my 'diverted' life and business. Serving others to find solutions through being a friend and business owner has allowed me to make many connections and given me an immense purpose again. What I have also noticed is that what you give out comes back to you. How amazing is that!

In order for people to feel cared for and appreciated, as a business owner, I need to add value to their lives. Being aware of what value you can give and even stacking it into multiple values makes you more appealing to others. Due to the pandemic I took my business online and now have business connections across the world. I also mentor people in Passionate Marketing and share the importance of following your passions. My passions now provide the GPS for my life and business.

I find that passion provides power as you are focussing on what excites you. It leads you to your purpose. It comes with a price as consistency and commitment are required. However, it is an amazing thing when your career and passion come together. Leading you to be an attractive person to others that can then add value and solutions to their lives.

The fixed mindset has been changed by following my passions and my business is moving forward in ways that I had not expected, and I can see huge progress and advancement.

As well as following my passions I have identified that:

• I have needed to learn to be authentic to myself but also to others.

• I have to learn to love myself through promoting and undertaking self-love.

• I have to stop listening to the wrong voice (nicknamed the Villain Within)

• I have to learn to value, lift and inspire myself and others.

• I have to learn to be consistent.

So where is my road trip taking me next?

I continue to work in multiple income streams that add value to my client's lives and I am still a network marketer. Through the mentoring process I support others to move away from bombarding their friends and family and instead lead with their own voice and passions. I continue to educate others around their finances helping them to plan for themselves and their family's current and future needs.

I also aim to raise awareness of PTSD and the stigma which can be associated with having a mental health condition. By encouraging people to find their passions they will start to undertake fulfilling activities and build their happiness. They will become mindfully aware of what makes them feel better and follow that route.

I regularly take time to reflect how much my life has changed. I could be bitter and stay fixed in my attitude and mindset. However, despite the PTSD journey having many trials and tribulations, they have helped me to become a better version of myself. I know that some of the best days of my life have not happened yet and I am excited for the next part of the journey on my route.

So, if you have got stuck, needed to or even chosen a diversion embrace the change. You will become stronger, wiser and even more beautiful through that growth mindset. Consider your passions and what makes you happy and fulfilled in life. Access support, develop self-love care practices and be authentic to yourself, in order to value and love yourself as well as others.

As a business owner, you know the value and solutions you can provide and deliver them with the right intention to the right person at the right time by being a massive person of value.

Arnold Palmer is quoted to have said 'The road to success is always under construction' so wherever you are today be grateful and keep moving forward.

BIO

Liz Ranger Is a director of her company ARISE that she runs with her husband Andy. They live in the south of the United Kingdom. They provide financial education and services to their clients in the UK for their business and home.

Liz is a mentor for online business owners and network marketers through Passionate Marketing.

Liz is also a mentor for the Accelerating Women Enterprise (AWE) through Portsmouth University. AWE deliver support to address the gender entrepreneurship imbalance through training and mentoring.

Liz runs her own Facebook group to love, value and appreciate others called Unique Love.

Arise Ltd – www.ariseservices.co.uk

6

THE JOURNEY INTO SOUL-LED BUSINESS

Kate Tolson

O pportunity-spotting, business acumen and quick action-taking served me well from day one of my working life, and through launching five successful opportunity-seizing businesses over thirteen years.

However, this success formula seemingly fell apart the moment I began work that felt like 'life purpose'.

What I didn't know at the time was that the formula was supposed to fall apart. What I came to learn was that your heart-led, purpose-filled, mission-driven work requires your whole-self to show up, and not just knowledge, intellect and action.

I started my first business in 2003 while working for a Fortune 100 company. I found buying business attire very frustrating, as unlike men who could visit just one of many business suit shops, women would have to spend hours and days visiting multiple clothing stores searching through the limited workwear lines hoping to find something that would fit their shape and size.

This first business idea landed perfectly within my mind, a national chain of stores, selling just the workwear lines from multiple international clothing brands. So that women, just like men, would be able to walk into one store and buy a new business suit.

Over the next decade or so I would come to learn that many fully-formed ideas that 'land' in our minds, are merely a catalyst to set us on a forward-path to guide us to other more aligned opportunities.

It was entrepreneurship that was beckoning me, not this idea.

The next year in 2004 I left my corporate job for entrepreneurship. While researching that 'fully-formed idea' I discovered a different opportunity, e-commerce, a brave choice back then. There were very few businesses selling online at the time, no supportive infrastructure yet in this fledgling industry, yet e-commerce was about to boom, I felt it and I wanted in early.

The opportunity excited me to be one of the first, to be an outlier, to take the risk.

So at the age of 25 I started my journey with entrepreneurship. I sold that business in 2008 just before the world recession (alongside a second business I had created), and started my third business shortly after. Again short-term, opportunity-driven by acting quickly on a perceived market gap. A couple of years later, I had an award-winning photography business.

Five years into that business, something changed.

I had had great success but inside I began to question whether I was in the right work. I excelled at what I did. I didn't have to market, my diary was fully-booked years in advance, I'd honed in on my ideal client so I loved working with the people that booked me. The work was enjoyable and easy, but something niggled inside because it just didn't feel like it was the thing I 'should' be doing.

In work I was always looking outside of me for inspiration and opportunity, in the absence of truly knowing what I wanted to do in my life. In 2015, certain life events caused me to look within, I was aware of a little spark within that had been quietly waiting for me to notice it - and that became the first step towards what I really desired to do.

I soon found that I'd made myself a 'golden cage', creating work that I was really good at, in which I had lots of admiration, recognition and amazing feedback that made me feel secure. I was earning well, I had a great work-life balance, my parents were proud, 'on paper' it was perfect.

I was comfortable in my 'zone of excellence', I was outsourcing time-consuming tasks which helped me streamline my workweek to 12 hours a week so had lots of time with my children. My diary was booked out for years ahead.

As time gently passed this inner-spark was becoming a flame. My purpose was beginning to ignite.

More and more I started to look within instead of looking around me in my work, I found that what I really wanted was diverging away from what I already had, and what I already did.

I started to realise that I'd gotten so distracted by opportunities over and over again, that I'd ignored and now lost sight of the signposts throughout my life pointing towards what I really wanted to do and why.

Instead I'd followed outer-opportunities that gained me approval and acceptance and created a false-sense of ease, security and comfort in my life.

It was time to listen to my heart for the first time and to create work that felt like it led to what I really wanted in life rather than what I thought I 'should want'.

By this point of realisation I had thirteen years of developing new businesses under my belt.

It never occurred to me that it wouldn't be as straight-forward as it always had been to act on ideas, to act on opportunities with this new work. To slot into market gaps, to act quickly and use everything I already knew how to do.

What unfolded for me next were the most confusing and frustrating years of my life. It felt as if I was suddenly a novice again, having to learn everything from scratch.

It took time to realise that something very unexpected happens to you when you commence your purpose-led work. That your mission-led business is not an opportunity to be created, it is an extension of who you are as a person.

It is not, and cannot be separate to you like an ordinary business can be. You cannot become a persona within this work. You cannot simply strategise and walk the steps with this deeply aligned work. You have to embody it, every single step.

What emerges through the lens of embodying your mission-led business is all of your unresolved 'stuff', your unhealed 'baggage' and those parts of you you have suppressed, it all unfolds right in front of you, in your work.

You suddenly have to battle through weeds in a garden that you have been ignoring, that have overgrown and run amok and those weeds are all right in the places you need to plant new seeds for your new work.

Your unconscious patterns and limiting beliefs suddenly emerge one by one and are growing right in your way.

It was confusing and quite perplexing to someone who'd got over a decade of entrepreneurship, under her belt. To do the simplest tasks I suddenly felt I had to move through so much 'stuff' to do them.

Self-belief wavered, my mind wandered, I struggled to express myself and get visible. I felt like I was energetically wading through treacle every single day.

I was often watching others emerge with the same idea I had been trying to move forward on for months, others would just run with it and have great success - while I was standing still and stuck. Not quite able to open my mouth and speak, to take my turn, reluctant to be seen and promote myself. Unable to ask for the sale for the first time in my working life.

Procrastination became my work colleague, perfectionism stopped me from releasing great work out of fear of getting it wrong. Because now getting it wrong, in work so close to my heart, was too much of a risk to take. Being rejected when you are deeply embodied in your work, feels like it would be the end of the world. Whereas in the past, in opportunity-led work, getting it wrong was just an opportunity for redirection, a choice to try something else.

It felt like I had at last discovered what I was 'designed' to do in life, and in doing that I had closed invisible doors right in front of myself. It became the biggest personal growth journey of my life because its success mattered deeply to me.

In the struggle I began to question if the resistance meant I was doing the wrong work, but in my heart I knew this resistance meant that this was exactly what I should be doing.

So I started the inner-work. Every time I stepped forward and began to understand and work through each limiting belief within me, I unlocked one of those closed doors of resistance. Limiting beliefs programmed within me in childhood, in school-life, in early work life, in my family patterns, were waiting for me to rediscover them and to let them go.

Every time I unlocked a door and stepped through it I noticed that I magnetised aligned opportunities in my unfolding work. With every step forward I took in that inner-work, an outer changed-experience unfolded to reflect the changed-belief within.

It soon became clear to me that the inner-work itself was the mission.

In this releasing process I was creating a roadmap to find success in aligned work, in purpose-led work.

I was noticing the resistance that appeared in heart-led work which was not present in opportunity-led business. I began documenting the journey and discovering powerful tools to help, discovering keys to open all of those doors and learning powerful lessons along the way.

Life-purpose work can be as simple as creating a roadmap of your journey through something difficult, and sharing it with others a few steps behind you on the same journey. It can be as simple as sharing the keys and the tools that helped you through your biggest challenges. For surely that is why we have the unique and varied challenges that we individually experience.

Standing now, eighteen years into entrepreneurship which started following opportunities and moved into embodying a deeply-held mission-led business, I've come to understand this. You can be very comfortable in an opportunity-led business, but you can be deeply fulfilled in a mission-led business, and that process can become not just a healing journey for you, but a healer's journey to serve others in a profound way, leaving a legacy behind you.

Your purpose in your work is to share from the heart. To share what you know through experience. To share what life has placed in front of you which you have problem-solved and unlocked closed doors to.

We all have different doors to unlock.

We all have different life-puzzles to solve.

There is no mystery. When you open that last door, you just need to look in your hands and see what you carried through with you, see what you have retained, what you have bought forward with you on your own journey and share that with others.

My own roadmap and keys created an online group programme to help mission-led entrepreneurs.

So if you have made a change from opportunity-led business

to something that feels like an inner-calling, but are struggling and hitting inner-resistance.

Ask your heart the question, is this resistance redirection? Or is this resistance a sign that the success of this matters so much it is triggering everything within you so you can see it and clear it out of the way. So you can become all that you are meant to be to do this work because it is exactly what you came here to do.

BIO

Kate Tolson is an Energy Coach and Rapid Transformational Therapist who helps heart-led entrepreneurs quickly find what is blocking them from moving forward with their mission-focussed business.

Kate works online with a global client base and has developed a strong reputation within her field. Clear to Grow Your Business™ is her signature group programme developed to help change-makers, creatives and healers to move quickly through unconscious resistance to creating the successful business they desire, while collecting their own keys to opening up their mission and vision along the way.

Energy Gardener – www.energygardener.com

7

EVERYTHING HAPPENS FOR A REASON

Jeannette Jones

L ife is a big adventure around every corner, when you are a teenager!

The world is your oyster, nothing can stop you, you know the score? Then life starts happening.....

I am a firm believer that everything happens for a reason – My first job in 1987 I felt was totally due to this! I had gone to the USA for a month to stay with a penpal, no parents with me and only just 16, so I was defined as an "unescorted minor". Long story shortened, I was stopped and fined when I should not have been, escorted through security to see my parents (for the money £50 was a lot then!) escorted back. On the way home I told my parent's what had happened, they rang and complained, it was investigated, refund, apology and an invite to be shown around for the day. At the end, I was told about an employment trawl they were doing, applied, interviewed and got the job with Customs and Excise (so many other stories I could share with you!)! 17 years later I had to leave due to personal issues. Best 17 years all because I was stopped incorrectly!

During this time I did the marriage, two children, divorce type of scenario but I also got diagnosed with multiple sclerosis (MS). My GP signed me off work for 3 months to get my head around it. At the time, I wondered why. I soon appreciated it as it gave me time to think that I am not going to sit in the corner and do the "woe is me" act, but "Bollocks!" (or similar!) life is for living and just get on with it.

I continued working for another 7 years and then signed off with ill health retirement. Shortly after, I became a Grandma, somewhat earlier than I had expected!.... I kept the "everything happens for a reason" philosophy with me and accepted that this is the direction where I would be heading.

I took the responsibility of being a Grandma very seriously – I can remember mine, I adored her. She was always there for treats and being the pacifier when things got a little tough. I loved staying over with her, although I can remember the bath in front of the open fire and no central heating!!!

Anyhow, this led me down the path of thinking about what I could do to make a difference for my grand-daughter. I realised that I already knew it had to be something about improving her future. With my health as it is, I knew I could not go down the route of my "own" business outright, so I looked at MLMs' (Multi-Level Marketing). These are often poo-poo'd and to this day I don't understand why. I looked into MLMs' which were in the eco business. I came across Wikaniko.

(We-can-Eco) and it ticked all my boxes – every day eco friendly, ethically sourced, "stuff" for everyday people! I signed up and that was over 4 years ago now.

What I love about being involved with this MLM is the amount of support which is available for me. There is training online, which explains about the business side of things. There is always support and advice either in Facebook groups or at the end of the telephone. So, although Anygreenwilldo is my business and I can promote it in the way I feel comfortable, I have the backup of a business which has been going for over 10 years.

Before the lockdowns which Covid gave us, I used to go and do events. I love people, speaking to them, finding out about their eco path etc and that is how my business worked. Obviously Covid brought an end to that, but I still had support and ideas from other members of Wikaniko which helped me adapt and evolve.

MS is not the 'best' sort of condition to have! I was ill-health-retired because of my fatigue. I get tired because of stress, I mean this is proper knackered tired, can't walk, write, all I want to do is sleep. I have even fallen asleep sitting up in a pub….. We all know that we should try and avoid stress in life. But I do, I only worry about what is important and if I can do something to rectify it.

Obviously when having your own business, you expect stress, but I don't and I can do more because of that. My sleep pattern is dire and my best time of day can start at 4am. I don't argue with me, I accept it and get up. Many emails are sent at this time of the morning, I schedule posts, I reply to any emails or messages that I have received the prior day. My day normally ends at lunch time, and I try to avoid networking and conversations from about 3pm as I get tired thinking!! – honestly, and then I can't remember words and it all goes down hill!! I still have not found an online networking group which starts at 5am – perhaps I could start one? There must be other business owners up at that time of the day surely!!?? Being at home working allows me to have a nap when I want, time manage my day, have a list of things to do and do the important ones. If I don't finish my list, it's fine I will roll over to tomorrow with it. It doesn't matter, I have done what I can today.

I have decided that, due to my health (and Covid) I will not be doing very many "proper" in person events now. I struggle with the set up/ down, sitting, standing – well virtually all of it! So, as everything happens for a reason, I have spent time, well a very long time actually, investigating who my ideal client is, creating a presence online, primarily Facebook and trying to focus my energy rather than the spag bol on the wall type (the scattered approach or headless chicken mode).

Being a business owner, you have to evolve. If you stay still, you will get over taken. I try things and sometimes they work and sometimes they don't. Either it is a bad idea or it could just be the wrong time. A couple of years ago, I created "Grab and Go" bags. So for £20 you got a bag of products that would allow you to clean your bathroom, or clean you etc. I thought it was a brilliant idea, but not really so with my customers. My current initiative is sample boxes. A collection of 8-10 samples from my shop. I had been doing them as a mixture of personal and home cleaning. Then someone says "could we have a sample box just for the kitchen or the bathroom" Of course I say….. sounds very familiar I think!!!

I know that I have already made a difference to many people now, my ripple effect. If I drop down dead tomorrow (hopefully not) I know that I have made a difference. Not to the extreme level of Sir David Attenborough but to family environments and to our future. I am still learning how to listen to my body, I try and slow down and not do everything at once, I know that I am going to get worse but I am not sitting back and waiting for it, I will continue doing what I can, in the way that I can. As I am in the MLM I have a team which is growing, so I do get commission each month from this. This really does help me financially, so if I have time for resting (haha) I do still receive an income. But I don't do it for growing a team, I do it for making a difference.

I still don't know how to judge if I have made it or if I have reached my goal? I don't know what my final goal is? Should I be setting targets throughout the year – should they be physical things like I have sold "x" amount of sample boxes, or I have had "x" amount of visitors to my website or "x" amount of likes and shares on my Facebook page? How can I know that I have reached it? I am not trying to take on the Worlds' problems, but I must know somehow that I have succeeded.

This business is the thing which is keeping me going. I always have time for my family as they are what is important – not that I could have a big flat screen TV or a new car on my drive every 3 years. Material things do not make me "buzz". Helping to make a difference to those who I know and love does. Without a healthier environment, it doesn't matter what else you have, you need your health.I suppose the one thing I have learnt is adaptability. It is my business and I run it as best as I can. I listen to my body, work how I can, when I can, but the most important thing is I love it as much today as I did when I first started! Who knows what tomorrow has in store for me, but I don't worry about it as "everything happens for a reason".

BIO

Jeannette Jones created Anygreenwilldo to confirm to people that doing something is better than not doing anything. She is a firm believer that people ought to take responsibility for their actions and that everyone and anyone can and do make a difference. There is always a choice and it is making the right choice which is important. It is not hard but changing your habit to allow future generations to make a new healthier habit is all it needs to make the difference. A healthier world starts at home.

Anygreenwilldo – www.anygreenwilldo.co.uk

8

LIFE'S TOO SHORT!

Teresa Rogers

My story is probably like many women out there. Classic corporate career, working hard, earning a good salary, climbing the 'ladder' of success, and slowly but surely putting family, friends, and personal life as a second priority to my job. Then came the redundancy – my own recommendation to the company I worked for, and the right decision for them, but meant I was out of a job.

I'd toyed with the idea of starting my own business the last time I'd changed jobs, a few years earlier, but hadn't been brave enough. Yep, brave enough! It takes an enormous amount of courage to start your own business and hats off to anyone who takes the leap. Those who haven't done it might be heard to say it's 'an easy life' or 'it's not a real job', but boy is it the hardest thing I've ever done. A business start-up needs courage to know they can make it, know that the loss of a regular monthly pay cheque is ok and know the freedom running your own business creates is worth all that hard work.

But it wasn't even the redundancy that pushed me to start

my own business. It was losing my dad to cancer. The timing of my redundancy was "perfect" because I was able to spend the last weeks of my dad's life with him, and for that I am hugely thankful that I was made redundant. But, of course, as with most devastating moments, it gives us a different perspective; we see things through different eyes. And, boy, was it ringing in my ears that "life is too short". My dad was only 63 when he died.

That was it!

That was the push I needed to know that a big salary and fancy job title didn't bring me happiness – it brought me stress, anxiety and, quite frankly, I was just a grumpy wife, daughter, sister, and friend to those people who really mattered to me.

And there was born my first baby – On The Spot – I was actually running my own accountancy practice (read: brain exploding emoji!)

My inner voice

Picture this, sweaty palms, shallow breath and a sick feeling in the pit of my stomach, thinking 'why on earth am I putting myself through this' – this happened in the moments before my first networking meeting back in 2015 when I started my business. As I sat there trying to work out how to get out of my car and walk into the meeting, it didn't feel like any of the years I'd been in corporate life prepared me for the immense nerves, fear, and imposter-syndrome emotions I was feeling.

But finally, it was time to start my own business, right?

Well, if this feeling ahead of my first networking was anything to go by, I was having second thoughts. How was I supposed to meet people and get my name out there to win clients if I couldn't even bring myself to get out of the car?

I vividly remember thinking how I could gracefully excuse myself, by emailing the organiser with just 15 minutes to go before it started. Maybe the nerves were really sickness, and I was coming down with something. Maybe, "something came up" and I couldn't make it (please let something come up, I thought). But I couldn't do that, and it wouldn't have been fair to the group if I'd bailed at the last moment. So, with my inner voice screaming "don't do it... save yourself", I told it to "shove off" and got out of the car and walked towards the meeting. The whole time remembering that the people I was about to meet were probably in the same boat as me, just starting out, and would be nervous too. But, if not, they would still remember the feelings of being nervous at their first networking meeting, so would be friendly and make my experience as comfortable as possible.

Val, the organiser of the meeting and Sarah, the incredible lady who took me under her wing that evening will always be remembered for their kindness and reassurance. After that I never looked back.

That networking event was the first of many to come. Network, network, network. I'm not saying the nerves stopped, and that the feeling in the pit of my stomach didn't show up from time to time, but it got easier... a whole lot easier with every meeting. And I spent many weeks and months building my reputation.

"Know, Like, and Trust" became the mantra to grow my business into the success it is today.

Who is going to buy from me if they don't know me? Who is going to want to work with me if they don't like me? And how will I grow my business if I am not showing up consistently in small business networking?

Working on my business

After all these years, I look forward to networking events. Yes, really! I, actually, look forward to them. Those fears back when I started have been replaced with excitement. Excitement for friends I'll catch up with (yep, going to networking repeatedly means you end up making some real friends), excitement for new people I might meet, and excitement for having time to work "on" my business, rather than "in" it.

And that's the thing. At the start of my business journey, with very few clients and all the possibilities in the world, I had bags of time to spend working "on" my business.

As my business grew, I could easily find myself working "in" my business for hours, days and weeks and suddenly realise I've forgotten to work "on" my business. Preparing a set of accounts, filing a tax return, or talking to my clients about their finances is incredibly satisfying. Loving what I do meant every day I was working "in" my business. And that's the easy bit, right? That's why we start our own business, to sell our expertise/talent, whether that's a service or a product, working "in" our business brings home the bacon!

But, working "on" my business is vital... in fact, the times I've pushed that priority to the bottom of the pile means I've stunted the growth of my business in the short term. Not looking ahead, strategising (ooh-er, big word alert) and planning where my business is going and how I can continue to grow it is super important time.

And when I gave myself that time in 2017, a light bulb came on and my second business was born. I'd spent the first two years networking like mad, building a trusted reputation among my clients and had grown to the extent I wasn't sure how to fit everything into my day and still maintain the value-based, client-focussed service and business I had built.

I sat having a coffee with one of my closest friends, Charmian, and asked if she fancied working with me to build a bookkeeping business. I'd found some of the work I was doing, was actually scope-creep on the fixed fee services my clients had signed up to. Always wanting to be helpful and never ever wanting to say no to clients, I'd managed to get caught up in many tasks that I wasn't being paid for. It showed that in many cases my clients really needed a bookkeeper. Yes, sure, I was muddling through, but not being paid and my clients not getting the best service because they weren't engaging the services of the correct person. It meant we were all losing out.

Now Accounting Services (back then, Now Bookkeeping) became my second child, this time with two parents: Charmian and me. Although, to be truthful, Charmian led that business and I just lurked in the background providing support where it was needed. It became the bookkeeping arm of our service provision, that eventually went on to offer payroll and other accounting services. It meant On The Spot could return to the stuff I loved, helping clients be as tax efficient as possible. Call me crazy, but I really do love tax!

It meant clients started to get a full professional service of day-to-day transactional bookkeeping support from a qualified bookkeeper and the regular reviews and annual accounts and tax expertise from me, as their qualified accountant. And I got some time back. Win-win!

Had I not made myself find the time in my crazy busy days to work "on" my business, it wouldn't have grown, and we wouldn't be where we are today with two successful practices and with an additional business partner who joined us in 2019, Laura, and an employee, Jennie – both qualified bookkeepers. And we plan for further recruitment later this year.

Time blocking

Sometimes finding the time to work "on" my businesses is hard... emails, client queries, tax deadlines, you name it, there's always something. That's why I now have to ensure I make time. Of course, there really are only ever 24 hours in the day and I do like my sleep and my free/leisure/down time – after all, what's the point of being your own boss if you can't be flexible with how you run your business – it means I can't magic extra time, so instead, I have to be more considered with it.

And what a difference time blocking has made!

The last year has been like no other. The pandemic has thrown every conceivable curve ball at us, personally and professionally (thank you, Rishi Sunak) but we are still here and have been running at maximum output for the whole time. It's meant as a team we have sometimes felt worried we might drop the ball on a deadline or piece of work. It's forced me to think differently. Time blocking and getting the right software to support our growing business has been the answer. Time blocking my diary meant I can plan important chunks in my day to achieve my priorities. Sometimes it has meant my diary looks a little hectic and almost overwhelming, so I now only do it for the day ahead; taking my to-do list and blocking specific times to achieve the most important ones that day.

It means I am sure to time block working "on" my business, amongst all the working "in" my business, client work, email answering – all the stuff I have to get done too.

Working "on" my business gives me time to stop and reflect – where we are, where we've come from, where we're headed, what needs to change and what plans we need to reach our next goal.

Future developments

I'm super excited for my next goal to create a passive income stream.

Trading time for money is the business model most service businesses find themselves in, but that means if we're not sat at our desks, working "in" our business, we aren't earning any money! I want that to change, or at least have a portion of the money pot to be generated from income that doesn't mean we're sat at our desks.

Ideas are in the making and to ensure I can make time to work "on" my businesses for this next part of the journey, I'm doing two things: I've joined The Accountability Club – to talk about my challenges, listen to other business owners and feel empowered to reach my next goals and I'm taking a course on how to create passive income to maximise our potential.

That feeling of knowing it's my business, my baby, where all my blood, sweat and tears have been shed means I reap the rewards, is like no other feeling!

BIO

Teresa Rogers has been a qualified Chartered Accountant since 2002 and has run her own accountancy practice since 2015. She helps small businesses to demystify the world of tax and use their numbers to bring life to their business story. On weekends, you can find her in the garden, in her craft room or drinking gin with her husband.

On The Spot / NOW Accounting Services – www.nowaccountingservices.co.uk

9

YOUR PURPOSE IS MY PASSION

Joanne Sumner

For Daniel
        You are a bright, brilliant spark of the universe. Not in some fluffy way. In a literal, physical reality, way. You are made of stardust. Energy can only ever change form, so you have existed as part of this universe before you lived in this body, and you will continue to exist in this universe after you leave this body.

Yet what we know, and what we experience right now so often feels more limited. More staid and set about with obligation and expectation. Living the life we want feels like a fool's dream sometimes, in the midst of providing for and caring for ourselves and our loved ones.

I know this from my own experience.

I was born into a highly controlling organisation; some would probably say a cult. Every aspect of our lives was controlled by a set of rules that were usually not explained (and

I mean, what time we woke up and went to bed, what we ate, what school we went to, what we studied, how we spent our leisure time, who we were supposed to - and for many of my friends did - go on and marry. Even whether we had children and every aspect of rearing those children too).

This control was exerted over us children in the name of giving us a head start in life. It was an experiment in producing leaders who would put spiritual principles at the heart of their decisions in all aspects of life. Explicitly seeking in the boys to create the leaders we would see in parliament, on boards of businesses, as teachers in schools, as leaders of families.

And in the girls they raised, the home makers who would sacrifice personal identity and ambition in pursuit of creating the right environment for the men and children to thrive.

Does it all sound like a cross between The Handmaid's Tale, Stepford Housewives and some hippy's dream? Because if so, you have got the right picture.

What this upbringing meant for me was that I was programmed to do as other people wanted me to do. The embodiment of a people pleaser. I was constantly taught to put others' needs first, to the exclusion of my own, to such an extent that it took me many years to be able to discern my needs, let alone meet them. Asked what I wanted, as an adult, I often had no answer because it was such an unfamiliar concept. There are times even now when I have to stop and consider, sometimes for a few days or even weeks before I can answer the question.

And yet, I had in me a small voice. The voice that insisted on marrying the man I wanted to marry, who rejected these beliefs at the first opportunity. The voice that encouraged me to apply to university and to study what I wanted to study even if it was half a country away. The voice that said, ultimately, NO. This is MY life. As far as we know, I only get this one. It is MY choice what I do with it.

Now, I doubt most people reading this chapter will have had

such an unusual upbringing. However, I imagine many people will recognise aspects of people-pleasing – putting other people's needs first, no matter the cost. Finding it difficult to say no. Struggling to set a boundary or to say when it has been crossed. Giving your energy to people who are in fact toxic for you. Not knowing what you want because you're not used to what you want being considered important.

That has been such a valuable learning for me – that my story is both unique and also not as special (for which read more dysfunctional than anyone else's) as I thought. Many of us experience the challenge of not knowing what we want our life to be or how we want to be. That is why it's so easy to follow other people's expectations instead – at least it's set out for you. Finish school, go to university, get a job, find a partner, settle down, get a car, get a house, have kids, repeat.

All over the world women and men are living this pattern and wondering why they are not fully satisfied. Many people ARE satisfied – and they are not the people for whom I created my business. I am delighted for them. The well-trodden path may be well trodden for a reason after all!

I am here to serve the seekers. I am here for the person running the risk of dying with their dreams locked up inside them. I am here for the person with the small still voice inside asking the question, "Is this all there is?".

I mostly work with women who have experienced success in their professional and personal lives. Sometimes outstanding levels. Yet they feel only partially fulfilled and the other part is niggling away. Maybe those niggles come out as physical problems that I help through yoga or Reiki energy healing. Maybe it is coming out as a feeling of dissatisfaction or listlessness. Maybe they don't even know. Things just don't feel quite right.

I recognise it because I have been there.

Fast forward through finding my first job, getting married, getting a car, a house and so on. You would find me on the outside a successful, personable young woman in a high profile and very respectable job. Miserable. As. Sin.

I was swamped by the job and didn't know how to ask for help; seduced enough by the profile to continue to sacrifice health for (apparent) social success. My marriage was suffering, and I lacked joy.

So, what happened?

One night, sitting in a supermarket car park, in the pitch dark because I had forgotten to shop for food, again. I turned to my husband and said, "I can't do this anymore". And by some act of grace, he responded, "Well if money wasn't an object what would you do?"

I will always be grateful to Neil for the power and permission of that question. In that moment, I knew that what I wanted to do was set up a centre for creative and healing arts. I had no idea how. I had absolute certainty though that that was what I should do.

A couple of days later I handed in my resignation and told my friends "You'll never have to listen to me moan about this job again! I've resigned and this is what I want to do instead".

You see, when you surrender to grace, with absolute clarity of purpose and openness about HOW, then things fall into place. One of my friends texted me back saying "Awesome. I know this is odd, but I have an interview at a Sculpture Academy, and I've decided that I don't want the job. I think you should come with me to the interview, and you should take the job".

I went to the interview, I got the job, I began to retrain in holistic approaches to health. My journey to heal from my upbringing and then from the imbalance of my life, and in particular to begin to value myself and my desire became the birthing ground for my business, Joanne Sumner Wellbeing.

I began simply. Each time I finished qualifying in a therapy or technique I offered it.

I knew how damaging perfectionism and Imposter Syndrome could be because I had experienced it. I had been swamped in my job because the terror of getting things wrong was so great that each piece of work took infinitely longer than it needed to. I had never been taught to think for myself, so how could I know what I felt was right?

I listed out pros and cons, weighed up arguments, and could never reach a conclusion because there was no standard, no internal moral compass to measure against. How ironic for someone who was working in the ethics of medical research involving human beings. I could see things from all angles and weigh in from none.

Slowly as I worked on myself, and as I trained, I began to discover who I am and who I wanted to be. I tried things out, and if they didn't work for me, I made it ok to let them go. Somewhere along the line I began to believe that growth comes through a process of trial and error over time. That perfection, being a fantasy, is not a goal worthy of pursuit.

Sometimes the work went quickly. I remember very early on in my business saying to my business coach, "I really want to teach Bach Flower Remedies, but I don't know how that could happen as I've only just qualified". A month later my tutor rang me to ask if I would consider letting her train me to take over the course.

Or the time one new year when I asked myself what I had most enjoyed the year before. Standing in the shower, I said out loud "I really want to do more radio". And three days later one of the stations on which I had been interviewed called me and asked if I would like to take over their wellbeing show as their presenter had emigrated to New Zealand.

When you surrender to grace, with absolute clarity of purpose and openness about HOW, things fall in place.

Other times the work has been slow. It's not easy to repro-gramme your brain, though it can be done. Learning that I had worth simply by being alive; that I never needed to help another person again and I would STILL have value, inherent value; that was hard.

And again, my journey may have its unique elements, but the results are not so vastly different. So many clients attach their value as a person to their productivity or their usefulness. Yet wholeness arises from understanding that you have value without doing, having, being or giving more. There is wholeness and healing in stepping off the achievement treadmill and allowing yourself to be present to this moment of existence right now.

After 15 years, evolving my business, I would leave you with these thoughts:

- Your ability to honour yourself is a gift. It allows others to honour themselves. So, use your yes when you mean it and learn how to say no when you mean it.
- Your dreams are worthy of pursuit. By surrendering control of exactly how they can be achieved, you allow the universe to surprise and delight you.
- You are a child of this universe no more no less than any other. You are loved by life itself.
- Every day, Life is conspiring for your good if you will let it. Even in the darkest days, where no meaning can initially be found, there remains a spark of hope.

Will you fan that hope and become who were you always born to be?

It is my passion to help you live your life of purpose and joy.

BIO

Joanne Sumner is a human potential coach, mindfulness practitioner, yoga teacher and energy healer practising in Winchester and running retreats across the UK. She brings wit, compassion and insight to problems that feel either insurmountable or ungrateful (do you recognise that "I *shouldn't* feel like this but..." syndrome?). Whether you come to a weekly class, book a treatment or a coaching programme, or attend a retreat, you will be met with love, compassion and total belief that you are creative, resourceful and whole.

And if you want a recommendation for a book that will change your life, it is Bronnie Ware's *The Top 5 Regrets of the Dying*.

Don't let your dreams die inside you. Let Jo help you create your life of purpose and JOY.

Joanne Sumner Wellbeing – www.joannesumner.com

HOW MY WELLBEING CHANGED THE DIRECTION OF MY BUSINESS

Cassandra Dartnell

Having spent 18 years of my working life in the corporate world I had reached burnout. I had been involved in creating large, themed events, corporate functions, and exhibitions across the IT sector, but I was done with travelling the globe, working long hours and dealing with the stress and office politics that came with that environment.

I wanted the freedom to set my own destiny. I needed a slower pace of life. I also wanted to start a family, but medical conditions meant it would not be an easy journey. Given this, I decided to leave the corporate world in order to focus on those events and clients that brought out my creative side, but which would provide enough flexibility as I went along the IVF route to starting a family.

So, in 2016 I set up my own events company, "An Eye for Detail Events" to support individuals, small businesses and event agencies with their event planning and onsite event support. I organised everything from community film screenings and fun days to weddings and wedding fairs, corporate dinners and conferences. However, I found that the events I was being drawn to didn't bring me the joy and the fire in my belly that I was yearning for.

At that time, I struggled to do everything I thought was needed to run a business. I was trying to be a jack of all trades, but I was mistress of none. I hopped about trying to deal with finances, strategy, marketing, website and content creation, social media, business development and administration, but it just wasn't working. I thought I was failing, but I now know that what I was trying to achieve by myself was just not realistic. We, as entrepreneurs, are often far too hard on ourselves and expect ourselves to do things that no corporate organisation would ever expect from one person.

In April 2018 I fell pregnant with twin boys. I knew I would need to be closer to home for the foreseeable future, so in the following months I developed the idea to turn my business away from providing corporate event planning and onsite support.

During the summer of 2018 I had my 'lightbulb moment' and I felt that urge to get that concept out of my head and see what other people thought of it. The idea was to create memorable events for women to connect, try new activities or learn new skills and have fun in new exciting ways and put themselves first for a change. Let's face it, it's something we really aren't good at and there are few businesses out there with this prime focus. It doesn't matter what stage of life we are in, we could all benefit from some 'me time' from time to time. Each event could focus around a celebration or a wellbeing retreat and would bring together bespoke memorable experiences for each guest to be inspired by.

I put this concept to the Hampshire Women's Business group on Facebook that very day, and the feedback I received was phenomenal. More than 25 small local businesses wanted to meet with me to talk through potential collaborations and over 50 women said what a fabulous idea it was! This is where my bespoke party planning idea started its journey and those conversations led to blossoming new collaborations.

Unfortunately, my plans were halted when I found out that one of my twins was diagnosed with a bilateral cleft lip and palate at my 20-week scan. I quickly realised that he would need a lot of special care in the first few months and would need two operations within his first year. I knew I wouldn't be able to continue this new venture for the time being. So, I told all my suppliers that I would return to work after an extended period of maternity leave, and I parked the idea for the time being.

I, like a lot of mums, struggled navigating my journey into motherhood following the birth of my boys in 2019. I battled with pre-natal depression for much of my pregnancy, and this worsened after giving birth to my boys. The juggle of managing twins, my son's condition, and the issues he had to overcome had a profound impact on my mental health. I struggled to leave the house, felt a loss in confidence in my abilities as a mother, lost any element of self care, as well as loss in my sense of identity.

As friends and family watched me deteriorate not knowing how to help, I finally pushed myself to reach out to my health visitor. I was quickly referred to some help through a local charity, Home Start.

Here I began to get the help I needed – a combination of medication and weekly support groups with other mums and home start helpers. The groups gave me the confidence to leave the house with the twins and learn valuable skills to deal with my depression and anxiety. It also gave me some respite.

It was here on these weekly sessions that I learnt the importance of 'me time', working out small ways for me to refill that 'empty cup' that I was living from. I introduced some small practices from trying new crafts, listening to audio books, to exploring the power of mindfulness and journaling. Slowly, by making these small changes, I started to see a shift in my mindset and my ability to cope better with life in order to help beat this anxiety and depression I had been battling with for too long.

It was strangely reassuring though, that the mums I spoke to on a regular basis, were all suffering from the same issues. but they always put the needs of their children before the needs of themselves.

When the boys were 3 months old, I went on a gift experience with my mother-in-law, a willow weaving workshop in the Surrey countryside. We enjoyed home-made soup, learnt this wonderful new skill making baskets and woven bird feeders, and enjoyed deep and meaningful conversations in the most beautiful surroundings. We connected with the nature surrounding us and little did I realise the impact it would have on me once leaving the workshop.

I went in feeling frazzled, sleep deprived, and exhausted by the feelings in my head, and I left feeling energised, more confident having learnt a new skill I had never tried before. I left feeling happy and relaxed, like I might have felt returning from a weeks' holiday!

This made me realise how important it is for us to look after ourselves and be a little 'healthy selfish'. It was at this time I wondered "just imagine how a day or weekend 'me time' retreat away with friends or colleagues would make you feel". A day with honest conversation, where we can feel empowered and confident in the way we as friends lift each other up, fill each other with smiles and laughter and a space where we can all collectively learn new skills or activities. It is proven that when we come out of our comfort zone and try new things our confidence, self-esteem and serotonin levels elevate.

This was the defining moment that I knew it was time to

launch the Bespoke Party & Retreat Planning Service. It was also the moment I realised I could really help people to deal with mental health conditions and improve their emotional and physical wellbeing. I was in fact the proof that it worked.

So once my son had recovered from his surgeries, I was then confident to relaunch the business and I started again in November 2020.

However, I realised this time around things had to be a little different and I needed to work out a way to outsource the practical elements of my business that I just wasn't good at or didn't enjoy. This would free up my time to do the bits I did enjoy. This shift has made a massive difference to my wellbeing and as a result I have had more time to produce a stronger project management, marketing, and PR strategy for the business. I have also been lucky enough to benefit from a lot of free training and mentoring through a programme run through my local council that supports small businesses. This has covered everything from the practicalities and legalities of running a business to detailed marketing and PR mentoring.

I reached out and explained my new revised vision back to the fabulous group of online female entrepreneurs on Facebook in November 2020. My hope was to reconnect more women together following the Covid 19 pandemic, allowing them to learn new skills and experiences, encourage confidence, and give themselves some well-deserved 'me time' breaks.

Since becoming a parent, understanding the element of being so time-poor, the constant juggling, the mental load that never shifts, trying to juggle a business or job, a home, a family, as well as trying to keep fit and healthy, I realised we too quickly put ourselves on the bottom of the pile when it comes to our wellbeing priorities. I was overwhelmed by the response that my post received –which led to many more fabulous collaborations with an array of amazing entrepreneurs who have now signed up to support this new venture.

So, let's talk about the impact of the Covid-19 pandemic. I realised during the first 6 months of lockdown that I was becoming more insular, not wanting to take part in family activities, or Facetime with friends and family. I had nothing to say, and felt utterly trapped inside my four walls, everyday slowly rolled into the next. Even now, as we start to navigate into our new normal, I still feel the pandemic has affected my confidence, my ability to socialise, my comfort level around others. Now I am seeing how it has impacted many of my friends and family too. I am hoping these events can help reconnect people both in person and virtually in a safe way and help people improve their mental health and wellbeing following this difficult year.

It has taken a good 4 months to put all the different packages together, with over 25 tried and tested suppliers. I have since re-built my website myself, taught myself Instagram, and executed a fabulous launch party in May 2021. Now the future is all about educating women, mums, entrepreneurs, and retirees of the benefits of our events and to spread the word of the importance of self care.

Having tried and tested our experiences I have become happier, more confident, and more social, something I really felt I had lost. Trying these new skills has given me a deeper appreciation of my surroundings, and the knowledge that you do not have to be good at something to give something a go for the first time.

The future is exciting. I hope to win more business, work to provide inclusive events, so no matter what your skill, ability, or accessibility you all can try a number of these activities and be involved in these experiences. I would like to achieve awards and be able to give back to a variety of mental health charities as we continually strive to help people become happier and healthier.

. . .

BIO

An Eye for Detail Events create memorable events that inspire your creativity, calm your mind, and bring you delight.

We bring together suppliers across Hampshire, Berkshire, and Surrey to create luxury, virtual and in person events for friends, family, and colleagues to reconnect and celebrate in style. All suppliers are unique because they can be tailored specifically to your event or celebration.

Perhaps It is a birthday, retirement party, hen party, baby shower or a Me Time retreat amongst friends. Or maybe you have a small business affected by furlough and you want to improve team connectivity and creative thinking.

An Eye For Detail Events – www.aneyefordetailevents.co.uk

YOU ARE NEVER TOO OLD TO START SOMETHING NEW

Sarah Sullivan

L et me take you back to June 2020. I was on furlough from my admin job at a small gardening landscape company. It was the first job of note I had had since having my children and I enjoyed being part of a team again and getting a bit of the old me back since becoming a mum. When the phone rang that afternoon and it was the company director my heart sank, I just knew it was bad news and sure enough they were letting me go. It was a small company and they needed to streamline as much as possible in these difficult covid times. I felt a real sense of loss - what now? I would really miss the office chat, the feeling of being useful and as my husband pointed out, the dressing up for work. In fact, come to think of it, I would really miss the dressing up for work! Every Sunday I had planned out my outfits for the week (Gok Wan does this as I explained to my bemused husband!) excited to wear dresses and skirts and even heels occasionally. Hmm that was food for thought....

A few days later my friend Claire called me, 'Sarah I'm stressing out I've got a Zoom call with management, what shall I wear? I've been working from home in my pyjamas'. I had often helped friends and family over the years with outfit dilemmas. I set to work putting together some suggested outfits with items I knew Claire had. We decided on a floral top with a statement necklace and bright lips plus her favourite jeans as these wouldn't be in view and she would still be comfortable. "Thanks Sarah you're a lifesaver." There was more food for thought.

Then one evening when the kids were in bed and I was engrossed reading some style blogs and scrolling through Instagram looking at my favourite fashion accounts it suddenly hit me – this is what I love! I mean I love researching the latest trends, I love putting outfits together, and I love helping people. Maybe this was something I could do for a living? I felt excited and energised but also plagued by self-doubt. At 48, wasn't I too old to start on a new path? But the seed was planted and the urge wouldn't go away. When I confided to my friend Claire that I was thinking of becoming a personal stylist but that maybe it was too late for a new venture, she told me, 'Sarah you don't realise it but you've been doing it for years. It isn't new you've always done it. It's just you've never seen it as a career'. She convinced me to at least look into it.

I'd like to tell you that from that moment I made a decision to become a personal stylist, but truthfully it was a lot more of a gradual process, because I was still lacking in self-confidence. The first thing I did was set up an Instagram account posting my daily outfits. It was nerve-racking putting myself out there and my posts were very rough and really mirror selfies with no filters, but I actually enjoyed being creative and it gave me a daily task to do and a sense of purpose, when the long days of home schooling were taking their toll! I was surprised by the support I received initially from friends and family, but then gradually from the support from other accounts who I was following. It gave me the confidence to keep going. The idea of becoming a stylist was still there, so I started to research training courses. I knew it would be important to get the grounding so I could help people properly, for example understanding different body shapes. There were many courses out there, many of them were online but the one I was drawn to was an in person course run by NHJ Style Academy. It was a four day long intensive course in London. I remembered Nicky Hambleton Jones from her time on channel four's 10 years younger and I admired her style and confidence. I signed up, using some savings, for the course starting in October. It was touch and go whether it would go ahead in these strange times, but as fate would have it restrictions were relaxed and in early October I travelled to London for my adventure. It was on day two I had a lightbulb moment. We had to pair up and conduct a personal shopping trip choosing two outfits for our partner, a day outfit and an evening outfit and then present them to the class the following day. I had a great time the evening before doing my research in the stores and collecting ideas for outfits. I met another friend Jo for dinner and she commented, "You're buzzing!" I really was! I felt like I was in my element. The next day I was so excited to get my partner to try on all the pieces I had selected. There were compromises to be made, she didn't like the trainers I chose, so we settled on flats, but overall I was so pleased with the outfits I put together and had really good feedback from the group presentation. As I headed back to the hotel that evening, I really felt happy and energised. I could really do this. The four days passed quickly and it was fantastic to be surrounded by like-minded people and learn from Nicky. I made some new friends and after completing lots of practical tasks, homework assignments and assessments I received my certificate at the end of the four days. I was a qualified personal stylist. I felt like nothing could hold me back!

When I returned home I felt slightly overwhelmed by what

was ahead. I decided to make a plan and take baby steps each day to set up my business. I started with the name. I wanted something that explained what I did and that included my name. This proved quite tricky as Sarah Sullivan is a fairly popular name! I had a good think about what I was offering. Essentially I wanted to help people like I had helped my friend Claire solve her styling dilemmas! So that's how Style Solutions by Sarah was born! A friend from school recommended a guy to help do my branding and website. He was part of a large company that normally only dealt with large corporate accounts but we had a chat and he said he would love to be involved in helping a start-up. One thing I learnt was that it is great to reach out to your friends and network of people you know as they are often only too happy to support and help. One school friend has displayed a poster for my services in his dry cleaners which I am so touched by!

Getting the website set up was so enjoyable and I am really pleased with the result. I still pinch myself sometimes that it is actually there and live! Once I had my branding and website I announced my new business and name on my Instagram page. I had already talked about doing the course and my trip to London and I wanted people to be involved in the journey with me for better or worse! I decided to be open about the fact that it was a massive step and that I had had feelings of self-doubt and being too old etc. Once again the feedback I received was so encouraging and people seemed to relate to these thoughts, many sharing their own experiences with changing direction or career. I let Nicky Hambleton Jones know about my plans and she was incredibly supportive. I was so proud when she told me I would make a great stylist as I had a 'good eye'. From here I needed to get my name out there so I got some leaflets printed and placed some adverts in local publications. I contacted everyone I could think of to let them know about my new business. I was enthusiastic and ready to go!

About a month later I came crashing down. We were still in the midst of covid and I was losing confidence with it all. The self-doubt had become quite crippling. I wasn't sure if I could do it but the gut feeling was still there that I really wanted to. I decided to reach out to a stylist I followed on Instagram. StevieB styled celebrities and had many years of experience in the industry. I noticed she offered style mentoring sessions. I got in touch and had three sessions with her. She was such an inspiration, she encouraged me not to give up and to look at all my achievements so far. My Instagram had grown to 3k followers and I hadn't even given myself credit for that. She gave me lots of practical advice such as giving more hints and tips on my Instagram, so people would start to see me as an expert knowing my stuff. She told me to contact local boutiques, introduce myself and talk about working together and to look at joining a business networking group. I also needed to practice as much as possible with family and friends. I began to get my mojo back and make a plan of action.

I joined the Hampshire Women's Business Group and that has been invaluable for sharing experiences and getting support. I realised that starting a business is a real rollercoaster and everyone is going through good times and bad times. I visited my local boutiques and introduced myself. I have made some really valuable connections and they have been so supportive, giving out leaflets etc. and in turn I have promoted them on my Instagram account and encouraged people to shop local and support small businesses.

I am also collaborating with a makeup artist – Lisa, and Sue who is a colour expert, more connections I have made through the business group. Now I can offer a package including a makeup lesson, colours and a styling session to customers.

I used the time over lockdown to conduct virtual sessions with willing guinea pigs! I received a photo and testimonial from a friend's wife recently who was so happy after our session. She was stuck in jeans and t-shirts as a stay at home mum but had a wealth of clothes in her wardrobe that she didn't know how to wear. Now she is mixing her dresses with trainers and her blazers with jeans looking fabulous. It was such a buzz to feel like I had made a difference.

So what does the future hold? At this point in time business is slow. I have had a few customers but I am still trying to get my name out there and there are still covid restrictions in place. It is easy to feel discouraged. Like everyone, the last year has not been easy but I'm still enjoying the journey and proud of what I have achieved so far. Vanda Varga another contact I have made in the networking group helped me come up with a strapline for my business 'Dress up, show up, be confident' so that is what I intend to do and inspire it in others also. When the customers come I'll be ready. For anyone out there considering a change of direction remember you are never too old and it is never too late. Who knows maybe I'll be sharing style tips with Gok Wan sometime soon – I'll keep you posted.

BIO

Sarah Sullivan is a qualified personal stylist offering a range of services in person and online. Wardrobe edits, personal shopping, style revamp, style revamp plus makeup and colours. Helping you to dress up, show up and be confident.

Stylesolutionsbysarah – www.stylesolutionsbysarah.co.uk

MY JOURNEY FROM CONFLICTED STUDENT TO CONFIDENT BUSINESS OWNER

Kate Browning

Very early on in life I realised that I was different from most of the people I knew, I wanted different things, had multiple interests and didn't fit into the 'box' that many people were happy to fit into. What I was being told at school, at college and then university was you had to pick something you wanted to do for the rest of your life, a career to focus on and then stick to that career for the next 50+ years. Now this just wasn't me and you can tell from my subjects that I studied at college that I had many interests and wanted to do lots of different things and was a natural entrepreneur.

For those of you that are interested I studied Geology – I wanted to be a Volcanologist, Fine Art – I wanted to do something artistic like Interior Design or Graphic Design, Business Studies – I was interested in running my own business, in current affairs and an office environment, Economics – I wanted to be a Financial Advisor as I'm good with money and numbers, Text Processing – I can now touch type very quickly – a good skill to have in any role.

As you can see the subjects I studied reflected my personality, my struggle between doing the sensible 'safe' subjects and the artistic side of me that wanted to create and be free. I was, and am to this day, a creative person, but I'm also analytical, very organised and great with numbers, which are two polar opposites! I was conflicted as it was drilled into me to pick one thing and do it forever and do you know what, I call bull to that! Who says you have to be one thing, do one thing, to fit into a specific box forever? Not me! Let me tell you about my journey.

I ended up doing a degree in Business Management which was the 'sensible' option however I have had multiple careers. I spent many years as a PA/EA/Office Manager which I always wanted to do and I did it – tick. I then went on to be a Wedding and Event Planner for a number of years, which again I always wanted to do and I loved it - tick, however you are pretty much on call 24/7, will regularly work 70 hour weeks in the summer months and you can say goodbye to your weekends. I did it for several years before I wanted a better work-life balance and wanted my evenings and weekends back, so I looked at a new career. Also my health had started to take a turn, I didn't know what was wrong with me and neither did the doctors, but something was up (it would be another 7 years before I got my fibromyalgia diagnosis).

Before I tell you what my next role was you need to know one thing about me, I've always volunteered and fundraised for charities since I was young. I love making a difference, supporting others and being part of making a real change. Therefore when I saw my next role advertised as a Regional Fundraising Manager for a local children's charity I applied without hesitation as it was a dream job. I worked for the charity for three years before I got to the point that not only was I working lots of evenings and weekends again, putting in way more hours than I should (because I wanted to make a difference), but I had also got to the point of having a string of not great managers, not just in this role, but in previous roles too. I was so fed up with working for people who were rubbish people managers, treated me badly, didn't appreciate me, I was exhausted and at a crossroads.

Since I was a child I have always wanted to run my own business, that was a massive driver for me doing my business management degree, but it had never felt like the right time to leave the security of a full-time salary with all the benefits like sick pay, holiday pay, pension, etc. However I had got to the point where I was ready to leave my job and when looking at other roles, the thought of having yet another rubbish manager drove me to the decision to take the leap into the self-employed world. That and wanting a better work/life balance, being able to design my own life, choose my own work, my own clients and have the flexibility that I was looking for, especially with the health concerns in the background (I still hadn't been diagnosed at this point, but was suffering badly with fatigue, pain and headaches to name just a few symptoms).

I am lucky that I have the support of my husband and a great network of friends who ran their own businesses and were full of advice on how to get started. But know this; when I went self-employed I had no savings, no business plan, no massive client list, not even a decent laptop. I started completely from scratch. I chose a Virtual Assistant business because of my varied background, I was naturally organised and throughout the various roles I had been involved with, I had experience in marketing, social media, design work, as well as project management and administration and I loved to create content and to write – hence why I am contributing to this fabulous book. So cherry picking all my favourite aspects of previous roles and putting them into a business where I could be my own boss was a dream come true.

When I set up my own business, for the first six weeks I was part time, then very quickly went full time. Because I had spent the last few years doing lots of networking for my previous role, I had built up a strong network of people who had got to know me, the type of person I was and they had liked, known and trusted me, so within the first six months I was at full capacity and back to working 7 days a week! This is not where I wanted to be, I didn't go self-employed to work long hours and lose my weekends, I realised I needed to make changes. I put a plan together, worked with a mentor, set proper goals, put boundaries in place and started the process of hiring my first associate. I had decided early on I wanted a team of Associates and not employees as it's lower risk and less responsibility and who knows maybe down the line I would have employees, just not yet.

What happened next is not something I expected or could have planned for. It was March 2020 and over the last month or two there had been reports in the news of a new virus called Covid-19. The government weren't too worried about it but I kept an eye on the news daily. Then when I was looking through applications for my first associate around mid-March it was announced we were going into lockdown. I thought my business is virtual so it shouldn't affect me too much, but how wrong I was. Within 2 weeks, 70% of my clients had given their 4 weeks notice to pause or terminate their contract. Everyone was panicking and cutting any expense and luxury they could and virtual assistants (Vas) are luxuries, so my business plummeted along with my income! It put a huge strain on my business along with so many other business owners.

The silver lining was because I have always been good with money and organisation, I had built up savings over the first 6 months of running my business, so it topped up my income to cover my bills and my husband was hugely supportive taking a lot of the burden. It took a good 6 months for my business to recover from covid and it's definitely different now, there is less stability, however I have two Associates currently working with me now and am on my way to hiring a third. I work 10am to 4pm most days and finish at 3pm on a Friday. I am working towards working 4 days a week by the end of this year, but earning more money and building a bigger team of Associates and then next year the aim is 3 days a week.

I love running my own business, I love the variety of work I do, I am now also starting to work more with purpose-led businesses who don't want to just earn money, but make a difference in this world, people who have the same values and ethos as me and it means I can once again not only earn a good salary, have a work-life balance, but I can make a positive difference to the people and world around me, which for me is essential to be fully satisfied and content with life. It makes me happy to make others happy, but I am not a people pleaser, it's more than that. It's having a sense of purpose, it's loving the planet enough to make real changes, it's respecting my fellow humans enough to make a positive impact in their lives.

The freedom and flexibility that running my own business brings is fantastic. Now don't get me wrong it is stressful, not having a set salary, going out into the world and winning your own clients, the lack of stability for someone who is a control freak, not having paid holidays or if you are sick and how you manage that, all of these are tough and you need to have a certain amount of resilience, but if you can do it and want to, then you absolutely should.

I may not be a Virtual Assistant forever, after all I am an Entrepreneur, but for now I love my business and what I do. I may evolve the business to be more of a business support hub, or a VA agency, or even turn it into a franchise, but for now Cherry Blossom Management is here to stay, it just keeps evolving.

What I love and have realised about running my own business and getting to know so many fantastic business owners is, you don't have to fit into a box, you don't have to behave a certain way, or do things how you are told, you have the flexibility to design your own life, what you want from it and how you go about getting there. For me it's been about the journey and not the destination. Yes I have goals of what I want to achieve and that will come, but if you spend your whole time focussing on the end goal, you miss the journey, the little highlights and moments that make it special. For me some of the highlights have been being a speaker at a global summit, running workshops on my favourite subject – Canva, being featured in a magazine, getting nominated for an award, being a guest speaker on a podcast and the feedback I get from clients when I make a real difference in their lives.

Taking that step from being employed to self-employed can be scary, but it is worth every tear, all the blood, the sweat, the sleepless nights, as the freedom it gives you, the life you can design for yourself, the self care and the relationships you build along the way are in my eyes, priceless!

BIO

Kate Browning is the Founder of Cherry Blossom Management. Kate and her team of Associates provide business, event and lifestyle admin support to purpose-led businesses, entrepreneurs and busy business owners giving you back time, freedom and choice. We specialise in administration, Canva design, content creation, getting you organised and time saving tips. You focus on what you love and we will take care of the rest.

Cherry Blossom Management – www.cherryblossommanagement.co.uk

YOUR DREAMS ARE LIMITLESS

Gemma Storey

You know the saying. Infinity has no beginning, and no end. But for my business there had to be a beginning – though, hopefully there won't be an end!.. At least not until I'm ready to retire to a Greek island surrounded by hundreds of cats by the age of 50.

I have been in business just over three years, and in just that short space of time it's been quite the rollercoaster of ups and downs, but it has been a wonderful and rewarding journey of self discovery, incredible friendships, freedom and valuable lessons. It has to be said that being an entrepreneur is very much like my favourite Miley Cyrus song, 'The Climb'. It ain't about how fast you'll get there, ain't about what's waiting on the other side. It's the climb. Now, I bet I've got that song stuck in your head, right? You're welcome.

I'm a firm believer in sharing your businesses story, as you just never know who you might inspire to go after their dreams.

So in that spirit, I want to dive in and share my entrepreneurial story with you.

My lucky break

In the early 90's I discovered Crayola crayons and that was the moment I fell in love with art, and so I started drawing when I was two. Few years later at school, I was encouraged by my year 3 teacher to nurture my artistic skills, which later won me an Art Scholarship. Fast forward to my early teens, I found a deeper love for my creativity at college where I learnt to combine art with computers and that solidified my creative path to grow my experience and curiosity in Graphic Design at university. When I graduated, I achieved 'Best Project & Student of the Year' - so it's safe to say I know my craft!

However, my journey hasn't always been rainbows and unicorns. Prior to starting my own business, I found it hard to break into the design industry without a degree. So instead, for a while I found myself floating from job to job, not really staying more than 2 years in each place. I've been a sales assistant, waitress, barmaid and beautician - which surprisingly, each one has taught me life skills I still use today. Although, I don't miss working the late shifts at the pub, as I came home with sore feet and clothes stinking of beer.

I eventually found my lucky break as I was scouted by a top design agency in Hampshire and worked for them as a Junior Designer. It was a real pinch me moment, as for many years I dreamt of working for this company and I really admired everything they created and often thought they were out of my league. Nevertheless, I strongly believe in the power of the mind as I used to have a photo of their logo pinned to my vision board, and would often daydream about working there. Visualisation, cosmic ordering, law of attraction - call it what you will, but it's such a powerful tool and you should certainly give it a try.

I loved working for the agency as it was a real taste of what it was like working as a REAL Graphic Designer on REAL projects with REAL clients. I was so fortunate to have worked with big clients from Google, Starbucks, Paypal, JP Morgan and many more. I gained so much knowledge and experience, which was an exciting start to my career. But all good things must come to an end.

The wake up call

Over time I started to become quite irritable and restless at the design agency. I started to notice flaws in their system and often questioned their ethics and the way they went about business, financially undermining their clients. I would sit at my desk, disgusted by their morals and a voice would creep in and say.. "You should start your own design business; you'd do a much better job!". Doubtful of my thoughts, another year passed, and I was starting to feel like a caged bird grinding away into the early hours of the morning, often working 16hrs days and weekends with no incentive or recognition.

My blood would boil seeing my directors and senior colleagues stroll out the door dead on 5pm headed to the pub, while us juniors were expected to stay on and slave away on projects we were told about 15 minutes before close, which was due the next day. The real kick in the teeth was when I discovered my male colleague who joined the agency 6 months later than me, had been given a £10,000 pay rise! I was the only female in the firm, and that was the moment I realised the gender pay gap really does exist. Feeling frustrated and hopeless at the fact I had no control over this controversy, I would bring my anger home with me often taking it out on my partner, Adam.

Most Sundays I would cry in the bath, dreading Monday at the thought of having to repeat my week over and over again with the same corporate bullsh*t. I would tell myself.. "But this is adult life right? We eat, sleep, work, repeat." Another unwelcomed thought would follow with, "You should be lucky you have a job, so quit your complaining!" I've soon come to learn we have inner saboteurs, and I like to call mine Regina as she is a mean girl - nowadays I pay her no attention.

One cold day in December with the run up to New Year, I woke up in hospital on a drip. I was there for three days with very ill health, and I later found out I had caught a chronic sinusitis infection which was caused by a mouldy air-con unit that hadn't been maintained or cleaned in years, which unfortunately was positioned right above my work desk! With my constant exhaustion and failing health, this was the wake up call I needed to leave and find a new adventure. At this point going solo wasn't on my radar, I just knew I had to get out for the sake of my health.

Shockingly, my letter of resignation was rejected as they couldn't understand why I wanted to leave, especially without a clear explanation of where I was going. I hadn't figured out my next step either, but I just knew in my heart it was the right decision and this was the first time in a long time I followed my intuition (I now call this my north star) A north star is your inner compass to finding your true purpose and happiness in life, always trust it as it knows the way.

Four weeks passed, and it was my leaving do at Prezzo (an Italian restaurant) and I vividly remember my drunk creative director stumbles over to me and slurs in my ear "Ya know Gemma, you can just come back to work on Monday as freelancers aren't successful, especially female ones". That was the moment I felt a fire rumble in my belly like never before and my inner voice screamed.. "Screw you! I can and I will - watch me!"

I packed up my pens and started out on my own – and that's

when Infinity Creative was born. I had a lot of nay-sayers out there who thought I couldn't make it on my own - including family members! But they became my fuel. I was determined to prove them all wrong, and show them that I could, and would, make a success of myself. That was back in March 2018, which makes me a pretty young business in the grand scheme of things. But I've worked with a huge range of wonderful female-lead businesses, learnt a lot in terms of process, best practices, and creative influence. I've also roped my fiancé Adam, who is a whizz with websites, to build the sites I dream up for my clients. My business gives me the freedom and creativity to build a life I am proud of - with no limits!

Injecting the magic

One of the biggest transformations Infinity Creation has been through is a rebrand. It might seem quick, but bear with me here. When I first started, I wanted to appeal to everyone and everything, like a lot of startups do. I designed myself a very generic logo and built a plain corporate website, and even though I didn't really like it myself (never a good sign), I went ahead with it. And guess what? I got terrible results from it. Because it wasn't authentically me, and it wasn't attracting the kind of people I wanted to work with. A no-win all round really.

So I gave myself a kick up the bum and joined Trudy's Happy Business 4 month coaching programme, which literally was a game-changer for me and my business. She taught me to embrace my weirdness and really showcase my true personality to my clients through my new branding. I had to let go of the fear of what people might think of me, and focus on the positive outcomes by sharing my fun and magical side with the world. Trudy also helped me to discover my niche in branding and position myself as the expert in my field, which is why I've lovingly coined a new nickname for myself as the Brand Alchemist, which feels truly aligned to my business and values.

Now I'm over the moon and in love my branding. I've attracted clients who think just like me, and who I love to work with. This is what I preach to my clients now. Be yourself, and just like the universal law states that like attracts like, you'll undoubtedly attract your vibe tribe too. After all, you can be the ripest and most juiciest peach in the supermarket, but not everybody likes peaches. And that's ok - so it's best just to be yourself. There's only one you and you have your own unique stardust and message to share with the world.

The sky's the limit

We have to remember our "why" when starting a business, and I feel a successful business is built on more than just wanting freedom and earning money. For people to buy from you, they need to feel connected and aligned with your mission and values. As Simon Sinek once said at a TedTalk, "People don't buy what you do, they buy why you do it". After I heard this for the first time, a light bulb went off inside my head and it changed the way I approached my own business as a whole.

Nowadays, I focus more on supporting my clients 1:1 through my branding and web packages, as my soul's mission in life is to inspire, elevate and empower women who are on their own journey of north star discovery and wanting to create a life and business of their dreams. Through this collaboration, I want to form a long lasting friendship, while being their biggest cheerleader in business by giving them the tools to be seen and thrive online. Building a business can be a really lonely and scary thing, so I believe it's important to surround yourself with ambitious and inspiring business friends.

In my concluding breath, I want you to know that if you can conceive an idea you can achieve it too.

. . .

BIO

Gemma is a Brand Alchemist from the realm of Infinity Creative, known for conjuring up the puuuurfect love potion to make you and your dream clients fall back in love with your branding and website again. With the help of her magic wand (apple pencil) and creative supervisor (Salem the black cat) she specialises in making you look good online and offline and will craft an authentic and star aligned brand that attracts your soul tribe and inspires them to make a magical and lasting connection with you.

Infinity Creative – www.infinity-creative.co.uk

14

FROM SMALL BUSINESS OWNER TO ENTREPRENEUR

Jude Wharton

I t's May 2010. I'm four months pregnant with our first child and my husband and I have just walked out of our new accountant's office with all the paperwork to show we have registered our brand new business with Companies House.

Starting our first business while expecting our first child may sound like interesting timing but the baby was the reason for the business. At the time my husband Chris worked as a Studio Manager for a medium sized web agency. He was often in London visiting high-profile clients and it wasn't unusual for him to be leaving the house at 5am and getting home at midnight.

I was a Workforce Development Officer for the local authority. I delivered and commissioned training and managed projects. My hours weren't as crazy as Chris', but I still worked full days. The role involved travel all around the South East region of the UK and it involved some evenings, weekends and staying away.

We knew we wanted to be hands-on parents when our baby arrived, we wanted to actually see each other as a family and for both of us there were other frustrations in our roles that we knew we would much rather not have to deal with anymore.

So, 2nd Floor Designs Ltd was born.

When we started 2nd Floor it was a very small, traditional web and branding agency. Chris took the leap into it full time straight away and initially it was just Chris working in the business. I worked in my job up until our baby was due, so we still had one full-time income and then I had my hands full with a tiny but very time-consuming person!

Chris was somehow getting clients, managing and doing all the work on the projects and keeping all the finances in order, while very sleep deprived and supporting me through postnatal depression. In short, he was amazing and to be honest, still is.

When our little one was a few months old we realised that the business was already just about working well enough that I wouldn't have to return to my job. We had thought that maybe I'd have to go back part time for a bit, to subsidise our income but the thought of it was clearly adding to my depression and we calculated that if I took on the project management, marketing and finance tasks, Chris could spend more time on paid project work to increase the income. The business was only 15 months old at this stage, so for it to already be in a position that it was, wholly financially supporting us, felt a bit scary but also really exciting. I felt so uplifted by the fact that we were completely in charge of our lives now. We didn't have any bosses to answer to and had complete flexibility over our working hours to spend time as a family.

I'll be honest though, that excitement didn't last very long for me.

I felt quickly deflated for a number of reasons. Firstly, Chris and I were both used to managing teams and projects and it took us a long time to settle into our roles, separate work from life and not end up bickering all the time. If you are trying to work with your partner or a family member, my advice would be to take the business out of the home. This made a massive difference to us. We got together with another local web designer we had made friends with and hired an office in our local town centre together. This meant we had to go to work, it got us into a professional mindset and most of the time a third person was there so the bickering couldn't happen. It meant we dealt with situations better, we naturally got more defined with our job roles and everything got a whole lot easier.

Another thing that got me really down was other people's perception of my role in the business. The attitude that I was just helping Chris with his business or that I didn't really have a proper job. I had a really good reputation in my career previously and it really bothered me that people didn't see the hard work I put in and how my role was key to the business.

I also had periods of time when I was very unwell with Lupus, Sjogren's Syndrome and Grave's Disease and I didn't like not being able to pull my weight. It was brilliant that I wasn't in my previous job anymore because I wouldn't have been able to do it with such serious flares. I had Lupus before I was pregnant but the flares were never that bad. When our little one was two, the other conditions were diagnosed and things got really bad for a while. The flexibility of having our own business was and still is amazing for me when I'm ill, but it's also really hard for me knowing that Chris has to work harder. I have no idea how people who run their businesses all by themselves manage when things don't go to plan in their lives. I really admire those who do it!

The third thing that affected me majorly were the financial peaks and troughs. All we did was project work, so we invoiced for each project at the end, or at certain stages throughout, if it was a longer project. If we had quieter months, the money didn't come in. We got to the point where we really could only cope in business for one more month and all of our money would be gone. That's a little bit scary when you have a mortgage to pay and a little one to feed. This was at a time where larger businesses still wanted a professionally created website or brand, but on the whole smaller businesses and entrepreneurs were going for the cheaper off-the-shelf DIY route for their websites.

We realised we needed to stop being small business owners and start being entrepreneurs.

We needed to get into the lower end of the market and ideally, we needed to do this in a way that brought in a passive income so that it could tick over while we also took on project work. We started creating WordPress themes for ThemeForest* and for a while they really took off. The money worries went away. Somewhere in all of this, we also had our second son, so I took a bit of a backseat again. But as more and more WordPress developers cottoned on to the theme industry, it became oversaturated and it was hard to make the same sales we had been. Around this time, we picked up a couple of clients who wanted us on retainer and so that kept us in a good position financially, with a recurring income and we could continue on our entrepreneurial journey of finding another more passive income while working on those projects.

This is when we started creating WordPress courses. This was really exciting for me. It meant I was using my training background again. We created a series of courses and a really good following through being in Facebook groups and answering questions, networking and putting tips out on social media but barely anyone wanted to buy our courses. Probably because you could get most of what we were teaching for free if you searched for it online. Everything being in one place in our courses wasn't enough incentive to buy. However, putting all of our effort into this wasn't in vain.

Through one of our retainers, we were getting a lot of exposure to entrepreneurs who weren't happy with their website. The well known DIY website builders didn't create a website that looked professional enough or high end enough for them, but they didn't need anything bespoke. One thing that was important for them was that they could easily make their own changes to their website. They needed some beautifully designed themes or templates combined with some awesome training tutorials and support. They needed everything we had done over our entrepreneurial journey in one reasonably priced package.

That's when Ready Steady Websites® was born. Our off-the-shelf website and membership site template service.

At the time of writing this, Ready Steady Websites® is just over two years old and it has grown more quickly than anything else we have done in our business. We really feel we have finally found the right thing to be working on. Something that people need and want and something that people tell other people about. It's something we feel excited about and want to focus on to push it forward.

Now, don't get me wrong. It's not like a Disney Princess film in our office where the sun is shining and Blue Tits chirp around us as we type. It's still hard work. There are days when we deal with someone inconsiderate or someone who just doesn't listen and then we wonder why we bother. When we have a quieter month of sales we wonder if that's the end of the idea but then we renew our efforts around networking, we create a better lead magnet, or advertise a new challenge and it all picks up again. It doesn't create passive income, but it does bring in a regular recurring income which is steadily growing and that has lifted a weight off our shoulders.

It has allowed us to be more selective about the bespoke

projects we choose to take on and has given us more time and flexibility to enter into collaborations with other amazing business people. Funnily enough, in the last few months we have embarked on three collaborations with other husband and wife teams. It has been lovely to work with others with a similar dynamic to us.

By moving into a more entrepreneurial mindset, rather than a small business owner mindset, we have given ourselves permission to have more fun with our business, care less about how others perceive us and we get much more out of it both financially and emotionally.

It took us nine years to finally create the thing that we really think is going to work and we've been in business for over 11 years. That's a long time and I am so grateful that we have been able to support ourselves through our business for that long to get to this place. There were times when that was only just happening, but we were determined not to fail, not to give up and we didn't.

So, if you are thinking of starting a business and wondering whether you are brave enough to do it, just give it a go. As long as you aren't scared of hard work and are in it for the long haul (unless you are very lucky it won't be a major success overnight), then just go for it but make sure you have someone to support you, even if it's a good networking group. I couldn't do it alone and I'm very happy that I've never had to.

*ThemeForest is an online market place for selling themes (designed templates) for WordPress and other leading website content management systems.

BIO

Jude Wharton is joint owner and Business Director of 2nd Floor Designs Ltd and the Co-Founder of Ready Steady Websites®. She is also the mum of two boys and regularly contributes to blogs and podcasts to talk about websites and online presence and also her experience of balancing life as a businesswoman with being a mum and suffering with chronic illness.

Jude's mantra is "Aspire to be the best in all the things you start, but in everything you do stay true to your morals and your heart".

Ready Steady Websites® – www.readysteadywebsites.com

15

ASK A BUSY PERSON TO DO IT AND
IT WILL GET DONE

Becky Stevens

That was me. Always busy doing stuff for other people and no time for doing anything I wanted to do.

I'd always been driven to succeed in anything I did and ended up in management roles in retail, working crazy hours that weren't good for family or relationships.

So when my husband suggested I be a stay at home mum I jumped at the chance - as I could do the stuff I wanted to do and spend all my time with the family.

But what did I want to do? It turned out that I didn't consider myself a very good stay at home mum, as I didn't like staying at home! It was boring, this mundane expectancy of "mum" duties. I found I had even less time to do the things I wanted to do - but what did I want to do? As our children got older, it was becoming apparent that I was bored and needed something more.

. . .

What I wanted to do

I started volunteering at the local primary school helping run their wind band. I hadn't played the trumpet in years, and although I had reached a high level with my music as a young adult, I never went to uni to study it or had any experience with children and music. Tentatively I started going along, showing the kids how to play their notes etc. Then I started conducting and before I knew it, I was arranging music for them, conducting in public, running after-school music clubs, and eventually running it solo.

In this time my passion for music rose from the depths and my hunger to play returned. I joined an orchestra and started playing and performing regularly. The conductor of the orchestra was quite strict with me in the first couple of years, pushing me beyond my comfort zone, and as an outspoken adult, I really struggled with it.

But I'm a busy person, doing one thing isn't enough, as I'm also someone who can get bored with what I'm doing if it's the same all the time! I explored other passions: silver and chocolate.

My love of silver started at the age of thirteen when my big sister gave me my first ring for my birthday. I then collected silver rings whenever I went abroad, and my jewellery collection grew – and it was obvious silver was the only colour I liked!! After several workshops as an adult, I refined my craft and started tinkering making friends and family jewellery for Christmas and birthdays.

Chocolate. My biggest weakness. There is always a plethora of varieties in my cupboard – as there really are different types of chocolate for every occasion!! Fruit and nut in the morning – because they're healthy! I've always had a sweet tooth, which over the years, my mother tried to curb. But she also made awesome tablet fudge and gave us sugar toast, so I don't think she helped my love of sweetness at all!! My mum's fudge however is something that I have only been able to recreate once - out of many tries.

And then I discovered chocolate-based fudge. Oh wow, the opportunities for flavour varieties with chocolate and I could eat it all myself! Well after a couple of trays disappeared, I realised I could not eat it all.

This continued and when our youngest started school, I was flitting. Making things, helping out in our village community, teaching trumpet, and generally saying yes to help others using my creativity and knowledge for free.

Be your own boss

We got a dog to help me say no, as I had a commitment to the dog. On a dog walk, I decided it was about time I showed my daughters that you can do whatever you want to do and be your own boss.

But doing what? The world of retail management where I had come from wasn't suitable for my family's lifestyle and I knew I didn't want to go back into that world in any form.

So how was I going to do this? How do I market myself without actually sounding odd!

Looking at the things I could do, I decided to focus on the things I love as that would mean that I love my work!!

Firstly, what do I love doing? Making cakes, making fudge, crafting, organising and running birthday parties, retail merchandising, making silver, playing and teaching music – the list seemed endless!!

By the end of my dog walk, I had chosen my 3 biggest loves, my 3 main passions that run deepest with me.

Why three? Because I'm a busy person, and I know my mind would be forever full of ideas for other projects and business ideas. At least this way, I could limit my ideas and be able to focus on different parts of my business at different times – after all, teaching is only really for 35 weeks of the year – what would I do in the other 17 weeks?

Then a name. Family WhatsApp groups are brilliant just for this! All sorts of silly ideas were thrown into the mix – but my middle sister quite quickly came up with "Silver Beats and Treats". Covering all aspects of my new business, but not limiting it for future growth either!

Having started out with two pupils and signed myself up for all sorts of fetes to sell my fudge and silver, I started a Facebook page. There it was, I was official!

Space soon became an issue. I was making silver on our dining room table. Our kitchen was overrun with chocolate, moulds, and packaging. Then the instrument growth started. First it was a keyboard, then two trumpets, then an upgrade to a piano in our lounge. Husband was triggered into action – the utility room was finally completed. I moved in and claimed it as my fudge den. He then built a dividing wall in one of the downstairs rooms and created me a workshop space. The instruments were still in the lounge.

Growth and focus

I soon realised that trying to do everything on my own was really hard. I hadn't a clue how to promote my products, my photography was basic, and my social media experience was limited – in fact, I really am a dinosaur when it comes to technology! Something needed to boost me or else I would just forever "play" at running a business, and it would eventually fizzle out.

I was invited to join a networking group – The Crazy Daisy Networking. I went along to my first session. It was a January. I was asked what my main aim was to gain out of that year. I knew what I wanted but I hadn't said it out loud. If I said my dream out loud in front of people that means I have to do it. I wanted to earn enough money to take my husband and our youngest to Cambodia to see my eldest sister. I was so nervous, and almost cried when I said my goal. But it was out there. I came home and booked flights and committed to paying it back monthly. I now had to ensure I made that money.

From then my business seemed to take flight; I was determined to achieve my goal. With the help of this awesome networking group, I gained knowledge and confidence. I was asked to help at wedding photo shoots – introducing a tangent into my business I had never thought about. I picked up tips, went to workshops and improved my knowledge and put it all into my business.

It was quite apparent that I needed to up my game and sort out the technology side of things! From no experience doing anything like this – I now have a website, various social media platforms and selling my products on multiple other platforms too!! I didn't do it all alone – my husband is VERY handy, and our teenage daughters helped with understanding social media!!

I reached my goal in my first full year and travelled to Cambodia in January 2020. I was beside myself with my achievements.

On my return I started a collaboration with Eternally Cherished, being their in-house silver smith and creating exclusive designs.

Teaching expanded from just teaching at home in my lounge, to teaching in a school. This came about as my mean conductor at orchestra, turned out not to be mean at all! He saw my potential and brought out the best in me. He knew I had it in me and encouraged me and supported me with the music side of it all. He then invited me to take over some of his trumpet pupils at the school where he taught.

Fudge was doing well, but more of a seasonal product, which has worked well while I settled into a routine.

. . .

Change glorious change

Then 2020 really got going with its craziness! Lockdown.

I thought my business was over. No more fayres, no teaching, no supplies for fudge. All my effort – gone. I wallowed for a week. Then started teaching online – a massive learning curve for all concerned. My online presence and perseverance were paying off and sales started to become regular.

From an idea I had in Cambodia, I created a silver jewellery kit that you can make in your own home. Then my conductor announced his retirement from the school, and I took over all his brass pupils – so I was to teach tuba, French horn, trombone, baritone and tenor horn. But I had to learn them first – queue more instruments to add to my collection.

With the events of the 2020 pandemic, my business has grown beyond my wildest dreams, and it has paved the way for expansion. My husband has got fed up with the number of instruments I have, my fudge den is too small for the ideas I have, and my silver workshop has become too small to work effectively in.

Now I'm being moved into our double garage. I will have a music studio that will have its own entrance and be just for lessons, practising and storing instruments! I'll have a silver workshop that will have secure storage – I long for floor to ceiling shelves so I can have everything I need ready to hand for packaging and drawers for all the silver elements I have. The fudge den is being expanded and I will have worktop space to expand my ideas.

I have changed so much running my own business, I've learnt that finding the right support is key.

I'm still busy outside my business, volunteering etc, but I limit myself and have learnt to say no. But whatever I do – I always get it done. However busy I am.

. . .

BIO

Becky Stevens is the owner of Silver Beats and Treats. She makes handmade silver jewellery and is the creator of beginner silver clay home kits. Becky teaches beginner piano and brass locally, nationally, and internationally. She also creates fabulous chocolate-based fudge for treats and occasions.

Silver Beats and Treats – www.silverbeatsandtreats.com

16

FINDING ME

Sara Quayle

Starting my business is a journey well trodden by many a new mother. Like so many wonderful women, starting my own business was about having it all (in a good way): flexible working hours, at least 2 days where I spent time with my babies and also not having to pay an absolute fortune in child-care, all while keeping my hand in and not losing what I had spent years learning and setting my own rules!

Sailing the seas

I left school at the age of sixteen with the intention of joining the Royal Navy (RN) as soon as I could. I had the support of my mother, which was helpful as she had to literally sign me away! I think this decision was quite easy for her as I have been told, but I can't believe, that I was a little naughty in my teenage years! So, the RN would be the best choice for me; I did not do well in my exams and literally didn't want to do anything but sail the seas. So, off I went to the Navy and very soon I passed out (completed basic training) and joined my first ship HMS *Invincible* as a Junior WREN Operator Maintainer Above Water Warfare. (Radar and Gunnery). I enjoyed it, can't say I was great at it, but I did my very best and lived the RN life to the full – might have visited many a drinking establishment across the world in the process – and by the time I was 23 I had been promoted to a Petty Officer.

I was now due some shore time and with a bit of luck and having a friend at the drafting desk (Hells Bells I can never thank you enough), I landed a job teaching firefighting and rescue techniques for shipboard fires at HMS *Phoenix*. Now the only problem with this job is that I had to literally stand up in front of people and teach, and I didn't think I could do this. The very first teaching session I had on my own I had to be "persuaded" out of the toilets where I had been sick, several times, with nerves! But once I did it and received some great feedback, my confidence soared, and I started to enjoy it!

I spent 3 years at the fire school and loved it so much, this was the experience I feel made me who I am now. Instead of going back to sea and back to my old RADAR days, I decided to leave the RN, leaving on a high instead of going back to something I didn't particularly like, plus I had just completed my Certificate of Education at Exeter University. I only managed this because a fantastic professor believed in me (remember I flunked my exams and only had a few GCSE's, no English or maths so taking on a degree course and being accepted was a slight challenge. Another person who had faith in me. Thank you Phil).

Life after the Navy

Since I found my love of instructing, I wanted to stay in this type of role. My first job outside the RN was teaching height safety and rescue techniques for harness users, predominantly in the construction industry. Here, my confidence flourished, and I learnt new skills and worked in some fab places including the construction of the Olympic Park in London and some memorable rescue training in a mine in Turkey! (Amazing what they did with a bit of rope!)

This job was full time and once I had my gorgeous baby boy, the early morning 0430 starts to work became impossible, so I had to leave my job to be a full-time mum. Two wonderful children later (Lara was 13 months and Elias was 3 years old) I made the decision to complete my NEBOSH (National Examination Board in Occupational Safety and Health) qualifications to update my knowledge and prepare to go back to work. I rejoined my old job, but this time only part time. Unfortunately, this did not work out for a few reasons, which rocked my confidence, but I decided to pick myself up and start up on my own!

Having to look after your family but still wanting to work is an emotional path that is full of guilt but, it is something that I knew was right for me – even though I sometimes question that, not because of my belief but the belief of others and the expectations of what a mother should be in other people's eyes! This brings in a level of doubt!

The doubt that I could succeed on my own has stayed with me and is a constant battle, although I have been running my small business for five and a half years! When I started out, I was doing quite a bit of freelancing. I loved freelancing for a particular company as this is where I met Bob. Now everyone should have a Bob in their lives. I will never forget him; he was my guiding light; he was the person who built me up, and he was the type of person who lifts you and makes you feel like you can do anything. Working for Bob was not well paid, but for the confidence and the opportunity to improve on my knowledge, it was priceless, Also, for my freelance work it has led to some great opportunities under my own company which is fab. Again, having someone believing in you is priceless and helps quash those self-doubts.

Feeling all at sea!

As you now know I joined RN at the tender age of 16; I look at 16-year-olds now and wonder, what was my mum thinking? I was so young, though I didn't feel like that at the time. I served for 13 years and loved and hated it in equal measures, the highs were travelling the world and the opportunities, the lows, the work, the distance from family and of course the very regimented way of life.

In the military you are told to obey the last order, you do not have to think for yourself, you just have to do as you have been trained and as you are told. This way of life does not set you in good stead to move out into the big old world and start a business. I was definitely not programmed to run my own business, so for me there was a lot of un-learning to do, especially around having your place in the hierarchy. I knew my place in the RN, but in the big old world, that type of class and hierarchy does not exist as much. I mean, have you ever had to call your boss Sir or Ma'am and salute them? I found it difficult speaking to people in authority as an equal, especially as an expert in my field when I was helping them – this took a lot of work to get my head around!

But some things have not changed, for which I am grateful: my can-do attitude, as long as it isn't knocked by others, I feel I can turn my hand to most things. Frequently, someone has asked me if I could provide certain training and my brain is saying NO, but what comes out of my mouth is a resounding YES! Not out of desperation of work (ok sometimes for this reason), but because my inner confidence and my desire to try something new gets the better of me.

Change and identity

Several things have happened to me since starting my own business. My confidence has grown, my marriage has failed, my confidence has dropped, my home has changed, and I have gone back to work full time. That doesn't mean that I am no longer a small business owner, I am, and I am still plugging away to make it work. Instead of having my business as my full-time work I have it as my side hustle, but it is still as important to me as ever. My business is a massive part of who I am, who I want to be and my journey here.

I am not exactly where I want to be at this time, but I am so excited for the future and feeling positive is a great place to be in. Listen to people you trust and don't do something just because someone else thinks it's a good idea – I got myself into a right pickle doing that. I had a great product in my online infant and child first aid course, but some people wanted me to do other things when my main focus wanted to be on this product, as I knew it would help many parents and grandparents. (It is proving popular). Another big mistake that is costing me not only financially but emotionally is something I signed up to after a phone call, this lady was very persuasive and told me some untruths, but by the time I had signed up to it the goalpost had moved, and I was tied in! This makes me angry even now! But I will learn from this and try not to be side-lined by others who are out only to make money. Making mistakes unfortunately is part of being a small business owner, it is what we do with their lessons that count.

The future is exciting, but I'm working on finding myself again (only 2 months from separating from my husband). I'm trying not to give myself a hard time for not being where I want to be, to trust in my capabilities, and start believing people when they say that I am good (I want to say "great", but I'm not ready yet!) at what I do. My biggest goal and challenge is to not get in my own way! If I avoid that, I know I will prosper.

BIO

Sara Quayle – Managing Director of Sara Quayle Ltd (Sara Quayle Safety).

Sara Quayle Safety helps companies and individuals with safety and first aid for work, home, and adventure. Delivering both online and face-to-face training and supporting families with first aid and household safety. Sara holds her CertEd from Portsmouth University and her NEBOSH in both general and construction. She also holds her SMSTS, first aid & H&S qualifications. She studied International Disaster Management at Bournemouth University. When not working Sara loves to run, she has a few marathons under her belt, spend time with her children, and enjoy great food and drink.

Sara Quayle Ltd – www.saraquaylesafety.co.uk

17

DRU CAN DO – SO SHE DID!

Dru Hawthorn

I'm Dru and I run a successful domestic and commercial cleaning business in Basingstoke and the surrounding areas, called Dru Can Do. I started my business back in 2013. I haven't always been a cleaner … but I have always been a doer, and I have always enjoyed working with people. I like being around folk and helping them, and that has been a determining factor in the roles I have chosen to do.

Originally I went to catering college and then I had a few different jobs in the course of my career. In no particular order: housekeeper, assistant manager of a pub, nanny, childminder, LSA (Learning Support Assistant) in a school, and finally, prior to setting up my own business, I was managing a nursery. I had done a bit of cleaning when my second daughter, Millie, was born in 2003, but it wasn't until ten years later that I decided to give it another go.

I was not terribly happy in my job as manager at a nursery

and knew I wanted a change of direction. A good friend of mine had set up her own cleaning business and was making a real success of it. She said just do it!! And I knew I could and that I would know what to do because of my previous housekeeping experience. This was in June 2013.

My friend passed me a couple of clients when the days they were requesting were already full or she couldn't take any more on, and I have literally never looked back. There was no big bang, no huge period of growth, no deliberate push to get bigger. I just steadily built up the business, gradually acquiring a good number of clients through word of mouth recommendations and via a Facebook page that I had set up. Even now, at time of writing, I don't actually have a website ... but it's on the list! And in those early days, it was still just me.

Then I got full, but I didn't want to start turning people away, so a friend came to help me out, firstly just for 2 days a week, then for 4 days, but before I knew it I was getting full again, so I needed to take on another person ... and now I have 17 cleaners on my team!

I started doing a gym in 2014/15, then a martial arts place, a 'dojo', and then I began to get some offices, plus a couple of community centres and village halls. By 2019 I had built up quite a number of commercial clients, and then I was approached to take on Dove House Academy School – 5 days a week – so at this point I had to take on some extra staff again.

And all this was (and is) still coming from word of mouth and FB recommendations, plus now also using the Nextdoor email service and going along (before Covid) to The Crazy Daisy Networking events. I know that I am good at what I do, and I train each new cleaner personally, bringing them out with me on jobs and doing the work together side by side, so that they all learn to do things the "Dru Can Do" way. It's important to pay attention to detail, to take pride in the work that we do, to be aware of each client's needs, and I want every member of my team to do the job just as well as I would do it myself.

I have built up a great team and I like being able to 'give something back' to the local community by offering flexible, part-time work, which enables mums who have kids at school to have a job that works around their kids and their family commitments. It also means I can offer work to people on benefits as they can take on a certain number of hours per week and be earning money, rather than feeling like they are completely reliant on the social security system.

For anyone who finds themselves out of work for some time, whether that's because of taking a break to raise children, or difficulty finding part-time roles to fit around school runs, it can massively impact their confidence. I have found that working with me can hugely improve their self-esteem and self-belief. I am absolutely over the moon that one of my previous girls has now gone to college to study psychology – because of the boost to her confidence she found from working at Dru Can Do.

I also love to see how much what I do can have a positive effect on my clients - how it helps people to feel houseproud again, feel tidier, cleaner, back in control. It is amazing how much a cluttered or out-of-control house can affect someone's mental health.

I remember going to meet a lady once, a potential new client, and I had never seen a person so on edge, darting about the place, apologising, whisking things away and saying, "it won't be like this when you come". Within a couple of weeks of doing her home I could see a complete change – she was so much more calm and content. She was like a different person. She had previously hated not being on top of the cleaning. She told me that once we were helping, everything felt so much better; she really saw what it was doing for her wellbeing.

I don't just mix and match and send any cleaner out to any

client. Each cleaner is individually allocated to each client, so that they can benefit from that consistency of service and build a good relationship. Several of my clients will have had the same cleaner coming to them for years now. And we offer a variety of services, bespoke to the client.

I really wouldn't want to do an office job, but I do like structure ... just not a 9-5 structure! I am definitely a people person, and I love being my own boss, able to be in control of my own life, destiny, and choices. And, believe it or not, I do still enjoy the cleaning! I find it very therapeutic.

I'm now on the cusp of wondering if I should stop being the cleaner and just run and manage the business? Is it time to take a step back and be the owner/manager instead? I hit my 100th client last month, and I am just getting busier and busier ... and still the enquiries keep coming!

In five years' time, I think I would like to see myself not physically working; not 'on the tools' any more, so to speak, but managing the business. And I can't really imagine wanting to retire! The idea of "doing nothing" doesn't appeal. Perhaps at the age of 75+, I could have several managers in place, across a number of local areas. I don't actually want to franchise – I would like to keep that sense of integrity that it's me, Dru, and that I am training each person to do things the "Dru Can Do" way. So, I think overseeing the business and placing managers in different areas, perhaps in a 15-20 mile radius around Basingstoke, is the direction that I would like to take the business. But I know that also means letting go – letting go of some of my oldest and favourite clients, letting other people go and DO the work so that I can spend more time working *on* the business instead of *in* the business. And that is something I do find difficult – I think that is just my mentality – I feel like I'm not earning money if I'm sat at home!

As well as being a business owner, I am also a wife and a mum. My two girls, Leonie and Millie, have grown up fast and are very strong, independent young women. I am also mum to four fur babies, my little dogs: Buster, Tia, Rupert and Charlie. I love the greeting they give me when I get in after a busy day, and how they will take turns to sit next to me on the sofa. I ran our local WI group for many years and loved bringing women of all ages together for a range of different activities and I feel that I made many new friends. I recently (just before lockdown) did a quilting course, which I really enjoyed, and I also like upcycling furniture. I've always got some little project or other on the go. I love cooking, especially for other people. When we have friends coming over, they always request my 'Hot Broccoli Dip': it really does taste amazing, even if I say so myself. And I particularly like making desserts and baking, things like proper old-fashioned cupcakes and butterfly buns. I guess I am just a doer, I don't fancy sitting around or watching TV, I like to keep busy and active. I do like to 'do' and that's why my business is called Dru Can Do.

BIO

Dru Can Do can do more than just cleaning – we are happy to do what the client needs us to do:

- housekeeping, for example making/changing beds
- putting washing on … or folding it and putting away
- ironing service
- taking delivery of online shopping and putting away
- deep cleans, spring cleans, end-of-tenancy cleans
- bespoke service as per client's needs

Dru Can Do Cleaning Services – www. facebook.com/drucando10

18

FINDING MY CALLING

Kari Roberts

I n a world where you are pushed to achieve academic success, seen as a failure if you don't, a culture where your every move is watched and each decision you make, or step you take, is seen as a reflection both positive and negative on your parents, is where you quickly learn to comply. So, a girl that has a zest for life and is full of love and fire slowly gets dampened by the world around her and by fear of the consequences if she doesn't do as she is told. Until, she finds her voice and ends up writing a chapter for a book on why she started her own business.

Despite so many years of self-doubt and a lack of self-belief, I raised a family and was lucky enough to float into different careers. Even though deep down I know I worked hard to learn, listen and say yes to every opportunity that came my way, eventually finding myself in a role that I perceived to be near the top of the 'success' ladder of the vision I had built. I had a great team, I was told I was leading well, respected within my field of expertise, my confidence growing even though I was sure one day someone would put their hand on my shoulder and say 'What do you think you are doing here?' and then laugh loudly in my face while showing me out the door!! Keeping me from venturing out on my own for so many years, a little critical voice inside me that I kept silencing but kept me stuck in my negative thought trap.

So, what changed? I'd love to say that I had a big 'AHA' moment where I discovered the confidence to set up my own business, but that was so far from what happened! It took a major transformation at work with a massive department restructure. My role changed beyond recognition and after the chaos settled, a flood gate of work rushed in and all the promises of a new team with training and a good support structure disappeared. I found myself falling into robotically working and the exhaustion of desperately trying to not feel and just getting on with the job. But of course, suppressing feelings never works. Sometimes when we are in the middle of something so unhealthy, we choose to be more comfortable with that rather than be vulnerable and courageous enough to get out of it.

That's until one sunny day six years ago, a day which started like so many had, with me juggling twenty different excuses of what to say when I rang into work saying I was sick but always ending up going in. That day I decided to take the afternoon off and drove up to see a good friend who, throughout the years, had been a great mentor. As soon as she opened the door I burst into tears. I told her everything that I was feeling and will never forget her exact words, "YOU HAVE TO LEAVE!!" She had never directly told me to do anything before, so these were incredibly powerful words.

COMPILED BY TRUDY SIMMONS

Becoming independent

My heart was in my mouth as I realised that I now had to make a difficult decision - I either had six months to get another job or set up an independent business? I decided I wanted to set out on my own. I started to put feelers out, but like most of my decisions and plans I left it till the last minute and again expected things to just open up when I left my job and the realisation hit - I had no idea how to start my own business.

The first two years were full of highs and lows, confusion and challenges. I had passion in what I wanted to do but no clarity and no plan. Then the inevitable happened, I was approached to work for a National Charity and took a paid role. My ego was stroked and I told myself it would only be for six months.

Two and a half years later I finally left the charity to fully focus on my business. My specialism was Parenting, but I started to fall out of love with the idea of my own business because I had an expectation the work would come to me, and it didn't. I hadn't worked on being visible to others outside the small circle of people that knew me, so I switched tracks and for the next year I worked with a coach building another business. This was a year of awareness, falling back in love with emotional strength and the science behind it and indulging myself. However, it still did not bring in any business, and I constantly rejected that voice within me telling me something didn't feel right. I kept getting drawn back to Parenting, but part of me felt I couldn't go back, admitting I had made a mistake and feeling like I had failed and that felt scary.

Reality then hit when I found out I was not clear on my offer, my message was getting lost, and people were confused about what I provided. I made next to nothing towards the end of 2019. I felt so frustrated and stubbornly held onto a path with no clarity of where I was going. Once again, I tricked myself into believing that I did not need a plan and that winging it with passion was all I needed. I created and launched courses with vigour and enthusiasm, only to have only one or two people sign up. It was so disheartening.

The exhausting middle

I limped into 2020 and thought my prayers had been answered after being approached to work with an online digital company to offer their Directors and Senior Managers Emotional Strength Coaching. They were struggling with supporting their virtual teams during the pandemic and the lockdown. At the time I thought this was my 'Golden Ticket'. Unfortunately it didn't turn out that way. My verbal conversation with the CEO about what I offered and the long-term impact I could make was really positive and I signed a contract, skimming through the terms which all seemed acceptable. However I missed one detail, which stated it would only be for a period of six weeks. It was a struggle to get appointments booked and the first two weeks were a lot of back and forth with Human Resources and trying to engage with Directors and Management. There was also a sense of mistrust around being 'coached' resulting in only half of the appointments taking place before the contract finished. While disappointing I am grateful for the opportunity and received some fantastic feedback. Finally, it showed me that working with corporations was not where my heart lay. One of the biggest lessons for me was to read every detail of the contract I am signing and not just go on verbal agreements.

However, I was very grateful for the income at that time as my small business revenue was grinding to a halt - my clients had started cancelling their appointments with the uncertainty of the time and my client list was too small to cope with these cancellations. During this time, I was lured back into supporting families through two local charities who reached out to me when the world stopped due to the pandemic. One wanted me to take a course they ran and create an online offering and run the pilot. Finally I felt I had the permission I needed to delve back into my specialism. It has been a long and drifting road but when you have a real calling and listen to it, it will keep pulling you back if you are vulnerable enough and have the courage to take the leap. Often you hear stories about the really bad times or the really good times but very few talk about those exhausting bits in the middle

I then noticed that Trudy Simmons, someone I had followed and admired, was starting a Mastermind. I saw the marketing at a point when I was seriously considering, once again, applying for full-time paid employment. I reached out and had a discussion with her and then decided this was the last attempt. Part of me wondered if I was employable and how I would manage back in the corporate world not following my passion and once again dousing the fire within me as I had done as a child. Trudy's expertise is clarity, and she didn't fail to deliver, - I got a lot of clarity! In fewer than three months I returned to my passion, supporting mums. I shed so much doubt and created beliefs around not going back, being clear on whom I wanted to work with, worrying about those I didn't want to work with and feeling like I was failing.

I refreshed a group I was running. I realised I had been playing small, only being visible where I felt comfortable, and feeling guilty about promoting myself at a time when so many others were struggling. What I did next was to use all the tools and knowledge that I helped and supported others with on myself. I find coaches often forget to do that! I nurtured myself, wrote journals, meditated and sat with unpleasant emotions, asking myself time and time again 'why is this stopping you?' There is true wisdom behind each emotion, remembering no thought, dream, result and emotion is better than another. I allowed myself to listen! I asked myself what I'd do if there were no rules or restrictions and how I'd show up differently? This outlook gave me a sense of freedom to take my baby steps. Recognising leaps don't work for me. I leap and then wonder how I got there and stumble with what to do next.

Growing a movement

Now I am coaching mums and creating more programmes, slowly growing a movement and providing a space where mums don't feel judged or inferior. I'm tackling the myth of what a mum "should" look like and the overwhelm and confusion that creates limiting beliefs.

The vast information on numerous parenting styles and the misunderstanding that we as parents have control over our children's future is overwhelming. I am helping them reconnect with who they are, their children are and doing what works for them. Most importantly I enjoy helping them to understand not to sacrifice themself for the sake of their children but showing their children to be secure with who they are, not feeling ashamed or afraid, that's the biggest lesson they can pass on.

And what about my lessons? I do have my goals and plans for the next steps allowing flexibility. I am looking forward to each sunrise. What the future holds for me is being able to work and play with ease and the flexibility of working from anywhere in the world. Outsourcing more of my admin work to focus on facilitating and coaching will make a huge difference. Always remembering to check back in with my WHY. I know how important it is to invest in myself and my business and know the value of having a coach who truly believes in you and wants to see you thrive. Every high, low and bit in the middle has been worth it.

. . .

115

BIO

Kari Roberts is a Specialist Parenting Coach. Building parents confidence to hold their children's hands and guide them to be secure with who they are. Co-creator of programmes; Parents Emotional First Aid, Building Emotional Strength and Feelings Affect Behaviour [online]. Over 15 years' experience working in health promotion, education and as a Parenting Expert for local government. Holistic coaching is at the source of my offer. One of my core beliefs is that emotional strength is key to living life fully and authentically.

Kari Ann Roberts Coaching – www.facebook.com/kariann2309

RUNNING THE GAUNTLET TO CHASE MY DREAM

Emily Laflin

Cut to January 2020, I was a Business Administrator for one of the best nursery chains in the country, Childbase Partnership. I absolutely loved my job and the company; I had found a role that I both enjoyed and excelled at!

And yet, there I was, standing face-to-face with my boss, handing over my letter of resignation. You're probably thinking, 'Well, you obviously can't have loved it that much!' But I truly did. It was not a decision I took lightly.

After having my second child, my maternity leave was coming to an end. Despite being offered the incredible incentive of 50% off childcare, the commute was a killer, and I had to make the decision that was right for my family, not just myself.

So, what was I to do?

I always had the vision of starting my own business, but the inspiration and opportunity just hadn't collided... until now. This felt right!

I am very fortunate to have a loving and supportive husband, and between us, we agreed I would have 6 months and £500 to get this business off the ground.

On 22nd January 2020, my dream became a reality – VIVA Support was born.

Having previously owned a recruitment agency for 3 years, I had a good idea of what did and didn't work when it came to winning new business. I was passionate. I was determined. I knew if I was going to do this, I would have to give it 110%. So, that's exactly what I did!

Terrified of investing money, I snapped up every free webinar I could, made the most awful DIY website, and designed my own logo. I was convinced if I ploughed money into the business, I would just end up losing it all!

I got on social media from the off, engaging on LinkedIn and in Facebook groups, using my experience to provide advice and guidance to those in need. Within 3 weeks, I had secured my very first client! It was a small job – about £70 – but it was worth a million pounds in confidence! I allowed myself to dream. I thought, I might actually be able to do this…

The contract was drawn up, and I was raring to go. Houston, we have lift off!

I was so excited to be up and running, but I wasn't getting ahead of myself. I knew there was a long road ahead but I couldn't help but feel optimistic.

Then, it happened.

Covid-19.

What seemed like a distant threat crept ever closer, all the way from Asia, into Europe, and finally onto our doorstep; a virus that changed the course of our lives in an instant. Cases and hospitalisations soared as businesses began to shut. The country stood still.

. . .

Lockdown.

Childcare and nursery became a thing of the past, with my two young children now requiring full-time care at home from me. As his workplace remained open, my husband continued to travel to work, leaving me at home with two children who now relied on me for everything, and a business, still in its infancy. When your business is just starting out, you want to react to everything at 100mph. You worry that, if you leave that email for 5 minutes, or you let that call go to voicemail, your business will crash and burn. I had to learn very quickly that something had to give.

I'd heard how common it was for people working from home to struggle with their concentration, motivation, and focus, but I was determined that wasn't going to be a struggle for me. I felt optimistic about the transition into a full-time, work from home set-up; however, I hadn't planned on having my two children as office mates...

In the new socially-distant age, my children were struggling to understand why they couldn't see extended family, play with their friends, or even shoot down the slide at the local park. At that moment in time, they needed me much more than my business did.

In the coming months, I barely saw my husband – we would pass like ships in the night. When he got home from work, I would pass on the baton, and he would take over with the kids. Meanwhile, I would go back to trying to figure out how on earth to get this business moving.

I was distraught. The happiness I'd felt, the positivity, the hope, was all ripped away from me, almost as quickly as it had come. Like so many, I was struggling to comprehend this new way of living. What was I supposed to do? How was I going to cope?

Then, struggling to breathe, my mum was rushed to hospital. Covid-19 had invaded her lungs.

I was lost.

I remember the intense overwhelm, exhaustion, and loneliness… it consumed me. At that moment, nothing else mattered apart from getting my mum home.

The odds were stacked against me. Nothing seemed to be going my way. The business was barely off the ground, how was it going to survive in the midst of this chaos?

Starting a business is challenging enough before throwing in the added stress of a pandemic, how could I possibly hope to succeed now? I didn't see a way forward. I couldn't see a way forward. I wanted to give up. I nearly did give up. But, in the darkest days, I found that fighting for my business gave me the greatest hope. Somewhere, deep within me, I found a strength I didn't know I had.

In May 2020, I invoiced £18, recording my biggest loss after a fresh cash injection to finance a new website. You could say it was unwise to continue investing given the volatile and unforgiving market conditions, but I simply wasn't ready to admit defeat – I wanted this.

Everyone was holding onto their cash, not wanting to part with it due to the unpredictable situation unfolding around us. This made fighting for new business an almost impossible task.

After a number of anxious days, my mum was finally able to breathe unassisted. Her gruelling stay in hospital came to an end; she returned home to start on her long road to recovery.

The UK infection landscape began to improve and childcare slowly resumed. Normality was inching ever closer.

June soon came and brought with it the busiest week since VIVA Support's inception. I finally had the space to think and breathe again; my hard work was paying off!

. . .

Growth

I was determined to be successful, so I invested in a business coach to help me gain clarity and focus. I set some crazy, ambitious goals to reach by the end of the year, which I laughed at – partly because they seemed unachievable, partly because they scared me.

I was gaining momentum.

I began networking (something that petrified me); I built my LinkedIn network; but most importantly, I started believing in myself. I was actually doing this. Yes, me. ME!

In July, I hired an assistant to support me with my social media, and in September I increased his hours and expanded his areas of support. To date, each month I have increased his hours further and further. Being able to support another person, from your own business, is such an amazing feeling!

My end of year goal, a mere pipe dream back in June, was reached a month early, before being eclipsed in December 2020. Since then, month on month, we've been reaching ever greater financial targets. I can't quite believe it; I still pinch myself every day.

Now 18 months on, there are two new additions to the VIVA Support team (and growing!). I'm still not entirely sure what the future holds for us, but one thing I do know is, I'm excited.

I have big dreams of opening an office, with enough space for several fully-staffed departments, each filled with industry experts, with VIVA Support being the default choice for ALL your business administration needs...

But for now, I am happy with being the go-to for HR and Recruitment administration.

If this journey has taught me anything, it is that planning will only get you so far – you cannot anticipate the unexpected. I'd be surprised if even the most organised of us had a pandemic on their list of eventualities!

COMPILED BY TRUDY SIMMONS

Much like writing this chapter, you don't always know what the end product will look like, but you'll never know unless you start.

A couple of years ago, I didn't expect to be sitting where I am today. Through it all, there's one piece of advice that has stuck with me: "if your goals don't scare you, they aren't big enough"

Always dream big! You just might be surprised at what you achieve...

BIO

My name is Emily and I am the owner of VIVA Support. We provide Remote HR, Recruitment and Business Administration support to Freelance HR Professionals who are at capacity, looking to grow their business, and increase their earning potential. We love helping other small business owners reach their goals and achieve their dreams.

Since its inception in January 2020, VIVA Support has gone from strength to strength, becoming highly regarded throughout the Freelance HR business world, and regularly receiving glowing recommendations from peers.

Throughout our journey, we have had the pleasure of meeting and working with some of the most amazing clients from a wide array of industries, forming both human and business connections for life.

VIVA Support – www.vivasupport.co.uk

20

HOW I BECAME THE QUEEN OF PIEROGI?

Ania Oakley

Thank you for taking the time to read this chapter, I am delighted and ever so grateful for being able to share my story with you and I truly hope that you will find some sort of inspiration or encouragement within these pages.

So firstly, a little information about me. I come from a small village in Poland, where going out to restaurants is a rarity reserved for special occasions.

I grew up in a house where food has always been cooked from scratch, with the aroma of my mum's cooking filling the whole house with love and passion. I always enjoyed cooking but never truly understood what it feels like to cook for your family, until I started my own.

I would often watch my mum making delicious food, and absorb her knowledge, care, and love she placed in it. It just felt like magic! She taught me how to cook without even realising it.

I believe that cooking at home is simply in my blood.

When people ask me what my passion is, I can proudly say that I have a passion for cooking, spreading love and joy through my dishes. So, with this in my heart I decided to follow this passion and so here is a story of Ania's Kitchen.

I believe that my journey started the day I became a mum in 2015, after having my first child, I was unable to go back to my full-time job and the only option was to ask to work part time, but this request was not approved. Therefore, together with my husband, we decided that I would stay at home with my two children (I had my second child soon after my first one), so here I am, a stay at home mum with two beautiful boys who I love dearly.

Suddenly I became responsible for two human beings with the consequence that becoming a mum meant putting my own life on hold and as we know children do not come with a user manual so my life was turned upside down pretty much overnight.

So, I threw myself into caring for my children and sadly, I lost myself along the way but don't get me wrong, I wouldn't change anything if I had a chance to go back in time. Well, maybe I would spend more time on myself, which I will talk about later.

When my boys reached school age, I suddenly had all this time to myself and strangely I did not know what to do with it, it was both an exciting and scary experience.

I had the feeling of wanting to achieve something for myself, to feel like a woman again, to put worth back into my life and not to just be a great mum.

These were just a few of the reasons I started my business.

At the beginning of 2020 I started working on my CV and applying for office jobs, deep down I was hoping that there would be nothing available because I felt no passion in returning to full-time work. I had done it all before, and it certainly is not what I wanted to do for a living.

One day, I was having a lovely conversation with my dear friend Serena and that afternoon when I went to visit her I brought along some home-made Polish soup for her to try. I love sharing my food with my friends and I wanted to give her an opportunity to try some authentic Polish food.

We were talking about food and suddenly she said that she could see how passionate I am about food. The moment she said those words something just clicked inside, I thought YES!!!, I AM passionate about food, about cooking from scratch, about sharing food with others, it makes me happy and proud.

Then disaster!!! Fast forward a few months and the world goes into lockdown due to Covid-19. This was scary! My husband (being a wedding DJ) was the first one to lose his job. We both started panicking, so I started applying for these jobs that I didn't want to do. Of course, there was nothing available, no one was recruiting. Maybe there was a reason for it? Lockdown made me reevaluate my whole life, my outlook on life. It made me slow down and appreciate the little things we do have; in a way it was an eye opener, I had my epiphany!!

My priorities and perspective on life have certainly changed. I became brave enough to follow my dreams and my passion, so in November 2020 I officially opened Ania's Kitchen.

Running my own business has certainly been a bit of a rollercoaster. At the time of writing this chapter, I have been in business for approximately 7 months, so I am still fairly new, and I know I have lots to learn and experience.

My first couple of months were exciting, full of enthusiasm, energy and drive but there were also times of doubt, fear, and stress.

A few more months into my journey and I started throwing myself into deep water and becoming more visible. I wanted to learn as much as I could as quickly as possible.

One of my regular customers introduced me to this

wonderful group Hampshire Women's Business Group which has literally transformed my life.

There is so much I've learnt through this group that I can not even begin to describe in words. I met so many incredible women, however, I am not going to lie, being surrounded by businesswomen became a little overwhelming. I started comparing myself to those who already had established businesses.

That little voice in my head became louder and louder. It told me to go back to my 'old and comfortable' life. Luckily, I quite quickly realised that this was just my fear speaking, not my reality.

I called this voice Freddie the Fear and I wrote a letter to him, in this letter I acknowledged him, and I thanked him for trying to protect me but I also told him to back off and that from now I am in charge.

Surprisingly he did listen, of course, he is very cheeky and keeps trying to come out every now and then, but he knows his place and he is reasonably happy to go back where he came from.

Running my own business has made me feel important and valued, knowing how happy my customers are gives me daily motivation to continue and improve on what I do.

I vividly remember feeling a bit lost at the beginning of my journey, I did not know what to do, how do I promote this business, what/who my ideal clients are, how to get visible and most importantly I didn't even know what networking was. I know - crazy right?

7 months into my business I have regular customers and a clear vision for the future of my business.

I dream about having my own food truck, so I can travel around the UK and spread love for Polish food, for cooking from scratch and love for my Thermomix.

I have met wonderful and passionate businesswomen who

have been on the same journey as me at some point in their business, so I stopped comparing myself to others.

They made me realise that it's OK to have all these mixed feelings, it's OK to be scared. I know I have support in them, and I truly hope that I can be of support too. Writing this is my path to giving something back.

Whenever I need help I am now happy to ask for it. I try not to do everything by myself because just like being a parent you need support, it is so easy to just burn out and to underestimate the amount of help you need when you run your own business.

I quickly learnt that asking for help is not a failure, it's a sign of wisdom. It's an incredibly important part of our learning and an opportunity to learn and discover new ways.

I also wanted to mention a little bit about self care. It is so important to always put YOURSELF first, it's not a sign of being selfish - it's quite the opposite actually. Just like when you are on an airplane, you need to put on your oxygen mask first to be able to help others. It's the same with our business.

If we want to be successful, if we want to serve people, we MUST look after ourselves first, so we have the energy that we need to succeed.

It took me years to realise this and believe me I still struggle with it, but self-awareness is the first step in the right direction, right?

Only last week I have realised how little time I gave myself for self care until one day I physically couldn't carry on. My body was sending me warning signals which I have been ignoring for a while, so I took a step back from my business for a bit, and I am recovering. I am currently away visiting my family, and I am enjoying every single moment. I know, when I get back home, I will be fully rested and re-energised. So, if you have managed to read this far, thank you and please remember to take time for yourself.

. . .

BIO

Hi, my name is Ania (Anna Oakley) from Ania's Kitchen
I cook authentic Polish food- Pierogi. For now! You probably wonder what on earth are Pierogi? Let me tell you, I call them 'little pockets of sunshine'. Filled with either sweet or savoury filling. Quite like Japanese dumplings-Gyoza. I am based in the New Forest and I offer a takeaway service with delivery to the local area. I am also an Independent Thermomix Advisor. Thermomix is basically the world's most powerful blender that also cooks and stirs. This kitchen gadget replaces 80% of all your kitchen appliances, saving you time and money. I am a proud owner of it and I use it not only to help me with my business but also in my everyday life.

Ania's Kitchen – www.aniaskitchen.co.uk

21

FROM CREATION TO FLIGHT

Helen Emery

I didn't have one of those epiphanous moments when I realised that I wanted to start my own business and even when it did finally sink in after several years of mulling it over, I had no idea what I wanted to do. Let me take you back…

When my son was born in 2015, I'd been an engineer for 17 years. I knew it was almost impossible to progress my career if I wanted to work part time. For me, having waited to start a family for so long, there seemed no point in having a family and working full time. It was at this point that a very close friend planted the seed of starting my own business.

Having no idea what this business looked like, I continued engineering and everything was fine with the world, until about eight months after returning from maternity leave, I had a miscarriage. The pregnancy was completely unexpected and the miscarriage itself devastated me. Post-traumatic stress developed into anxiety and depression. Later that summer I broke my ankle, which over the following two years would require two surgeries to put it right. I also seemed weighed down by migraines and ENT problems. All of which combined meant I never quite managed to settle back into the job I once loved.

Just before Christmas 2017, the idea for my business was born... I received a call from my son's nursery to say that the printed mugs we'd ordered hadn't arrived and that the supplier wouldn't deliver them before Christmas. As they were Christmassy handprints ordered as Christmas presents, delivery after Christmas was pointless. I found myself having to drive miles to the nearest pottery café and I thought 'there has to be a better way?!'

The day I took my son to the café, my seed-planting friend came too. On the way, I told her, "I have an idea, but I'm not going to tell you what it is right now." The three of us had a lovely afternoon and on the way home I told her "My business idea is to do pottery painting but mobile. No idea how, but I think it'll work." Her response, "Awesome!" And so, the idea for my business was created.

2018 came and along with it, another period of worsening anxiety and poor mental health. While the idea of a mobile pottery painting business was still there, I did not have the energy or confidence to do anything about it.

Towards the end of 2018, I realised that I had been working for 20 years and that in a few months, I would have been with my then-employer for ten years. Here was another alarm bell ringing. I didn't want to wake up in another ten years and realise I was still working for the same employer, without it being a conscious decision. I had to do something but I didn't know where to start.

2019 brought almost five months of physical health problems and just as they improved, we received news that no family wants to hear... Mum had cancer and she would start a course of chemotherapy the following month. This was a body blow to us all. Mum is the epitome of matriarch – always there, always strong. This was it. This was the 'life is short' alarm bell.

It was then that another good friend told me that I had to stop dancing around and that my dream wouldn't move forward without taking a leap of faith. She tasked me to go away and find out how much a kiln would cost. Nothing difficult but something I had to know. That evening, I sat down at my laptop to find out that very thing. What I found, however, said fate was intervening... I found a kiln supplier that I had passed many times on my way to work, who ran courses on 'running your own pottery painting business' and the next one was a month from that day! I remember being so excited and signing up there and then; thinking this would be the way to know if it was something I wanted and could do.

I attended the course and loved it. I came home and set about putting together a business plan, figuring out the logistics of running a business from home. I was feeling the added pressure of our son starting school that September and how we were going to manage childcare in school holidays with two working parents. This really spurred me on and so I placed a (sizeable) deposit on the kiln I wanted and worked towards getting it installed and commissioned before Christmas 2019. Which I did. Kudos to me.

Now, we all know what happened in 2020... I don't need to go into the ins and outs only to say that my business plan did not go to plan. I didn't finish work in July 2020 and I felt like my business limped through the year. And you know what, that was okay. We were all healthy and Mum is in remission, we still had jobs, income and a roof over our head.

In January 2021, I signed up for 'The Spectacular Challenge to £1million' with the The Daisy Chain Group. And then, the evening before we were due to start, the country was placed into its third lockdown. At this point, I felt very dejected. The thought of homeschooling, working and trying to inject life into my business so that I could credibly contribute to the challenge seemed insurmountable. But we were rallied, we were there encouraging each other and the following day I posted an advertisement on my Facebook page saying that despite the lockdown, I was still open for business. At the time, it felt like a throw of the dice. I'd posted adverts before and they had done very little. Oh, my, goodness. Things in the next 24 hours went a bit bonkers! My post was seen by an admin for a local group and she shared it. It was then shared on several other Facebook groups and suddenly The Painted Dragonfly flapped her wings and started to fly.

What happened during those first two months of 2021, proved to me that the business would work but I had to work smarter. I had been very reactive, believing that everything required my immediate attention. There felt like so much to do but not enough time to do it and I was paralysed by procrastination.

Things calmed as schools went back in March and I was able to take stock and have a look around to see what was going on. By this time, I was totally disengaged with work and it was a real effort to show up everyday. We were still working from home and I wondered if anyone noticed whether I was there or not. I decided that I would finish work in July, ready for the start of this year's school summer holiday.

One day was particularly bad and I sat at my desk unable to do the task in front of me. I went for a walk, came back and still stared blankly at my laptop. Later that morning I had a video call with my therapist and she commented that I wasn't myself. I told her how I'd been feeling and she asked what the difference was between me handing in my notice that day and in three months time. I thought for a moment and half-heartedly said about three months pension contribution and maybe a bit of savings. We talked a bit more and she suggested that I write my letter of resignation, tell my husband I was going to send it and see what his reaction would be. So I did. And his reaction was one of little surprise and essentially, if that was what I wanted to do, then he supported my decision and I should do it. I called my boss to tell him what I was doing. His actual response was "I'm envious". Within 90 minutes of that first conversation with my therapist, I had handed in my notice. I immediately felt about three stone lighter and about a foot taller.

I was amazed at the reactions of those around me. Family, friends and colleagues genuinely happy and excited for me and my future, most wondering why it had taken me so long to take this leap and all commenting on the happy demeanour I now displayed.

One month later, I hung up my hard hat and steel toe caps. I can honestly say that I haven't looked back. It is easy for me to forget that I ever had a day job; the pandemic has helped me adjust to working on my own. It can also be easy to forget that this is work; I am being paid for doing something that I love. The enjoyment customers get from the service I provide and the delight they show when they receive their piece of fired pottery fills me with utter joy. There is no other way to describe it.

Before 'Lockdown 3.0' success felt likely but now I feel sure I can succeed, so long as I am smarter about how I do things. I have always had a 'be perfect' tendency and I'm learning that done is better than perfect. I'm gaining knowledge and experience all the time.

Very early, the advice given to me was to concentrate on one thing at a time and get that right. Then build from there. People are often full of great advice but to take on board everything, you'll tie yourself in knots. I'm learning what I need and what I want to run my business, my way.

Right now, I feel like my business is in a building phase. In January, I was catapulted into a place where I was very busy but I didn't have the toolkit or the procedures in place to sustain it. I knew that it would work but I couldn't continue at that speed and with so little behind me. I will be the first to admit that I had no idea how much behind-the-scenes work there was to do; social media presence; customer engagement, learning that the customer wants to buy from 'me'; building a website, which I knew was important but I wasn't sure why; bookkeeping and accounting; and stock control. All this was on top of mastering my 'trade'.

Moving forward, I want to be financially sustainable in my own right and I have set myself goals, in order to achieve this. I don't want to be a 'hobbyist'. I want to be a role model for my son, for young girls and for other women: you can run a successful business and be present as a parent.

It's fair to say that life has thrown a reasonable number of lemons in my direction over the last few years. But I'm owning them and making some sweet-tasting lemonade, which I can sit and enjoy with those I love. Owning a business is giving me a freedom that I have not felt before. The future looks bright and promising, and I can't wait to see what each new day brings.

BIO

Helen Emery is the owner of The Painted Dragonfly, a mobile pottery painting business allowing you to create beautiful, bespoke pottery from the comfort of your own home. She lives just outside Winchester with her husband and her five year old son. Helen graduated from the University of Southampton in 1998, becoming a Chartered Engineer in 2005. For the last twelve years, she has worked as a civilian for the MoD and in April 2021, left to become fully self-employed.

The Painted Dragonfly – www.thepainteddragonfly.co.uk

22

FALLING IN LOVE WITH MY BUSINESS

Sara Thornton

S ometimes the hardest journey is the one most worth travelling.

It started with a romance, as it often does.

But while a lot of businesses are born out of passion for a product or service, my business started when I met my future husband, Jason. For years, Jason had been building websites for family, friends, friends of friends, and … well, you get the picture. He hated taking money from others – he just wanted to help them, so he did everything for free in his spare time.

When Jason and I started dating, I was watching him build a website one evening and asked if I could help. He showed me the building blocks of how it all fit together, and I began building websites myself. With some encouragement from me, we finally started charging for our work. People were loving what we were creating and enthusiastically recommended us to others. Our number of clients grew, and suddenly we had so much work that we could no longer fit it into evenings and weekends. We both left our well-paying day jobs to work on the business full time and finally took the leap to make it official. WebHolism Limited was born.

The road less travelled

Now, I wish I could say that it was all rainbows and roses from that point forward, but the reality was those first two years were the hardest I had ever worked in my life. I lived and breathed WebHolism, from the moment I woke up until the moment I went to sleep, 7 days a week. I had been so used to working for someone else, where you turn up, work for the day, go home and then your time is your own. Suddenly, there was no off-switch. No one telling me I could go home. No one to guide me or tell me I was doing a good job. For the first time in my life I was entirely responsible for my own income every month, and it terrified the bejesus out of me. I wasn't mentally prepared for this, but Jason was. He sat by me every day, keeping me sane, providing the support and encouragement I so desperately needed.

Neither of us were strangers to hard work (I had a degree in engineering, and Jason one in computer science), but WebHolism stretched both of us in ways we had never anticipated. Overnight I had to become competent in bookkeeping, our company's legal obligations with the UK government, business insurance, personal tax returns (which I'd never had to do before), and how to invoice, quote, and effectively run a company. Jason focussed on the heavy coding projects (being a programmer at heart), and I took care of everything else (being a control freak at heart).

Due to my lack of self-confidence, I vastly underpriced our work. The website industry back then was notorious for being secretive around pricing, except for the super cheap companies which shouted their "£99 websites" from the rooftops. I couldn't understand how they could build a good quality website for so little. It took me a long time to understand that the "£99 website" wasn't actually good quality, often came with a lock-in clause that meant you were stuck with that developer/company, and to top it all off, they would charge you a monthly fee for the privilege. Sometimes the domain would also be kept hostage, meaning that if a business owner wanted to leave, they'd have to start their website over from scratch, including finding a new domain name. I remember speaking with a high-profile developer at a website conference who boasted that his business was doing incredibly well. Struggling with our pricing, I asked him, "Oh wow, how do you do it?" He replied "It's easy, you build their website for a cheap deal, then you lock them in with a monthly payment, and if they don't pay, you take down their website. I took someone's site down just last week – they paid up pretty quickly, I tell you!" He chuckled at the memory. I felt sick.

Right then and there I vowed to educate and empower every single one of our clients and every business owner I could, so that they would never again be held hostage by a developer or website company.

We were already building websites that our clients could update themselves, so I started including a free step-by-step guide with every website we built, so our customers could easily make those simple changes that most business owners need to do at some point; update some text, swap out an old image for a new one, you know, simple things. At the time (over a decade ago), I hadn't realised how radical an idea this was. Most website developers and companies made their money by keeping hold of the website reins and charging their clients (sometimes extortionate prices) any time they wanted to make even the simplest of changes. This practice being so common, many business owners had no choice but to comply.

Over the years, our popularity grew and ever so slowly I began to increase our prices for new clients. One day, I was writing an email and suddenly realised that I hadn't been worrying about money. In fact, it had been months since I had worried about our finances. We weren't living a luxurious life, but we were comfortable, and our situation was sustainable. We had regular clients who paid us automatically each month – they were happy, and we loved keeping them happy. We worked hard, but it felt more manageable now. Things had eased, and we relaxed into a comfortable plateau. Finally, things had settled – what a beautiful, wonderful relief.

A gentle route through rocky terrain

Fast forward five years.

"Are we still going to be doing the same thing a decade from now?" I looked over the rim of my water glass to see my husband looking at me. It was a valid point and both of us had started to feel the itch of the plateau. It was an uncomfortable thing for me to admit because I liked security, and I liked things being reliable and stable, but those gentle words floating out of Jason's mouth hit me like a cannonball. I instantly saw the both of us a decade older, the wrinkles starting to show, grey in Jason's hair, and still doing exactly the same thing with the same clients. This wasn't necessarily a bad thing – I loved our clients, and I'd hit an easy, comfortable "lather rinse repeat" cycle where projects were easy to deliver, and problems were easy to solve. But the cannonball had struck home. I wanted to help more people but felt frustrated and overwhelmed by how few hours I had in the day. We couldn't take on any more clients – we were full.

Jason had been urging me for years to take on help to deal with our workload, but I was the queen of excuses: "We can't afford to employ someone else. What if they make a mistake?

It's going to take me so long to train them, it would be quicker to do the work myself", and so on and so on.

The truth? I was scared (with a heavy dash of pride, ego and control freak thrown in, of course). I was scared of change. I was scared of letting the genie out of the bottle and not being able to cram it back in again. I would go round and round in arguments with myself, until I'd scared myself into submission.

"What if I hired someone that I liked but was not good at the job – could I handle letting them go?"

"Are you crazy? I could never fire someone!"

"Aha! So that means I'd be stuck with them forever!"

"Well, that's that then. No way I can hire someone."

I guess, in truth, I was afraid of making a mistake. You can't regret something you never did, right? And then I was given an opportunity that I couldn't refuse.

My wonderful, conscientious sister (whom I trusted deeply and who was at least as meticulous as I was) needed some extra work. She had finally decided to pursue her passion of teaching piano as her main source of income and needed something to fill in the financial gap while she worked on building her fledgling business. Side-note: my sister has been an insanely talented pianist ever since we were kids – I would have done anything to help her make this a reality. Well, it was a no-brainer. I began teaching my sister the basics of building websites (much as Jason had with me, all those years ago). She had a natural eye for design and took to it like a duck to water.

When the pandemic hit a little while later, a good friend of mine (an incredible marketing director and gifted copywriter) had her hours cut to part time. Again, a complete no-brainer. I offered to train her up in SEO (a natural fit with her marketing background), so that she could help with some of our non-coding workload. She gladly accepted.

A mere twelve months before, the idea of hiring someone was too much of a lava-filled chasm for my brain to leap – the thought alone would set my heart racing (not in a good way) and make me all nervous and sweaty. But now I had these two incredibly talented women at my side (virtually at my side you understand, I mean we were in the middle of a pandemic and all), breezing through my backlog, and what's more, I absolutely loved teaching them.

I think that's what brought it home for me. I needed to share my knowledge with others. It had started out so innocently with those seemingly insignificant user guides that we gave out free to clients all those years ago. It progressed and morphed over the years; free online website training when handing over a new website to a client, providing answers to thousands of little questions from clients on how to do a particular task or about the basics of SEO, and culminating in teaching these two brilliant women the foundations of website design and SEO.

Free to create my own path

Today, my horizon expands before me. I no longer feel trapped within my business. I've climbed on top of this crazy ship and am finally steering it for the first time, rather than it steering me.

I get the honour of working with the most amazing clients, and the luxury of being able to choose who I spend my time and energy with. I still undercharge for what we deliver, but it's a work in progress and so much better than it was. I'm actually getting time to work on our own website, which is being launched later this year, along with a set of training courses that will empower business owners to be able to build their own professional WordPress websites, and also understand SEO and apply it to their business. At long last, I'm on the path to being able to help more people than I could ever possibly do in a one-to-one client relationship.

I'm finally starting to fall in love with my business. Not the heady rush of a new fancy, but that deep, enduring, secure kind of love that you only get with overcoming difficulty and coming out the other side rumpled and tired, but knowing deep down that you could face anything together.

And I've got to tell you: it feels absolutely amazing.

BIO

Sara Thornton is co-founder of WebHolism, a website and SEO agency, specialising in website and SEO strategy and training for small businesses, startups and entrepreneurs. Sara runs WebHolism with her husband Jason and they are cheered on by their adorable, adopted dogs Nano and Lulu.

WebHolism – www.webholism.com

23

GOING SELF-EMPLOYED
(VOLUNTARILY) IN A GLOBAL
PANDEMIC: I MUST BE CRAZY!

Erin Parnell

I just cannot carry on like this.

It is 4:30, still dark outside. The house is silent as I find my clothes that I laid out the night before. Creeping around, I get dressed and go downstairs. I feed the cats as I wait for the kettle to boil. I make myself a coffee, sitting in silence staring out into the garden, watching as the sun slowly starts to rise a little. I am tired; I am emotional; I just do not know how long I can carry on like this.

As I get in the car, it is chilly, but my coffee can keep me warm and awake for my 72-mile commute to work. As I drive on the motorway every overhead sign is telling me "STAY AT HOME", and I wish with all my heart I could. I realise after a while I am crying, and this continues every day and just will not stop.

The roads are eerily quiet, I barely see another vehicle on the whole 72 miles, which is normally cluttered with commuters and angry, tired drivers. Once again, overhead signs tell me "STAY AT HOME", and I wish I could just turn the car around and go home. No one sees me like this, crying as I drive to work. Almost all my friends and family are working from home or furloughed. I see all over social media people complaining about being bored or updating their houses with before and after pictures. In the meantime my partner and I are like ships that pass in the night. Handing off my daughter to one another for 4 months, all the while I am hiding my tears.

While driving, I wait until it is a decent time to call my partner so I can say good morning to him and my daughter. During the working days I see her for a maximum of 30 minutes a day, that is if I don't have a meeting or get stuck in traffic, then I might not see her at all. I can go days without seeing my daughter, even though we are in the same house.

I just cannot carry on like this!

I want to work for myself, running my own business. I have been working so hard for the past few years, so you know what, I am going to do it. I am going to put a date in the diary: "this is the day I will go self-employed". Regardless of the hurdles I may have to jump over, I will do it.

Where did it all begin?

When I found out I was pregnant, my partner and I were pragmatic about the whole thing, and we also knew we did not have a clue about being a parent or caring for a baby. We enrolled on a 6-week NCT (National Childbirth Trust) course where we met other pregnant couples. The course was brilliant and the lessons on breastfeeding were very encouraging. I told myself I was going to breastfeed and that was that.

Skip forward, emergency C section, hospital ward, completely out of our depth. The nurse pops my little one on my boob and she couldn't latch. All my plans and preparation out the window, I was devastated. I was crying when the nurse came back with a nipple shield, and long story short, it worked. Apparently we have flat nipples in my family, who knew!!

I could see the days counting down to when I had to return to work; I had 4 months' maternity leave. I had managed to stash quite a large amount of breastmilk in the freezer, which had been a lot of work, but I was proud of it. It reminded me of this special time I had with her, and I wanted something to remember it by.

I looked online for some sort of breastmilk keepsake for me to remember my special journey with her, found a company and was about to place an order, when I said to my partner, I am going to make something myself. There was a lot of trial and error, but eventually, I managed to find a perfect technique of preserving breastmilk so I could incorporate it into jewellery. Then my first proper piece, the purple heart, which is the inspiration for my logo, with an E in it for Elara. She is the inspiration for my business and triggered a creativity in me I never knew I had.

Stepping into self-employment, well more like jumping headfirst!

OK, so WOW! 2020 what a year, looking back it feels surreal, but most importantly we are here. We made it this far!

I guess the start to this year did not go as everyone planned. You remember that date I was on about, well it happened and now I am self-employed, as planned, despite the global pandemic. What does it feel like, I hear you ask. Well, simply put, it is terrifying!

I guess it is normally a big leap of faith to go self-employed full-stop, but to do it during a global pandemic may seem like utter madness. Maybe it is; I guess mad people don't really know they are mad, do they?

2020 taught me so much about myself and my business. It taught me that family is so important. I was too busy being caught up in the monotony of routine to really realise what I had been missing.

I went back to full-time employment when my daughter was 4 months old, and I had just launched my business. My partner took 5 months' shared parental leave. So, he had more time with her than I ever did, which at the time seemed amazing for him, and I did what needed to be done.

When I launched my business, I joined a few business groups and the Hampshire Women's Business Group (HWBG) was recommended. I joined as a bit of a lurker and made a few connections but stayed in the background a lot. Never really believing I was a businesswoman. Then in 2020 I told myself that if I wanted to be serious about making significant changes to my life, then I would need to be more visible, more present, and be more out there. This is not something that comes naturally to me; I am a confident person, but a natural introvert, so I like to sit back and observe. However, I cannot do that if I want to move on, grow and develop in my business and as a person.

I decided to try networking, which was ideal as due to the pandemic it was all online, so I did not need to go anywhere or find time for that. I didn't really know what it was all about to be honest. I developed relationships with people, got to know people on a personal level and even collaborated with another Hampshire based business, Silver Beats & Treats whom I continue to work with now. The HWBG community supports me, helps me, and they are my biggest cheerleaders.

I achieved a lot in 2020; I was nominated for various awards, a finalist for the Great British Entrepreneur Awards, a winner in the Women Who Achieve Awards, but my biggest success was gaining clarity.

The clarity for what I want my life to be like. The clarity for how I want to live. This year, being self-employed, I have launched a new business, re-built my website, added new lines, collaborated with new businesses, and rested.

Most importantly to me, I have been able to collect my daughter from nursery. We have walked home together every day, regardless of the weather. We have played; we have cooked and eaten as a family; and it has been everything I wanted it to be. Long gone are the days when I would see her for a few minutes just to say goodnight, or the morning telephone calls. Therefore, I tell myself, I will be successful.

I have already lost so much time I will never get back; I will not lose anymore. What is it like jumping headfirst into self-employment? Terrifying, but worth everything.

What does it mean to have truly "made it"?

Some people get gratification from reaching the next promotion, the next rung of the ladder, the next pay bracket, but when have we finally made it? What does it mean to truly have made it?

I guess for a lot of us it is a comfortable retirement or a directorship or a comfortable financial position. This is not the case for me. From a career point of view, I can keep going, keep climbing that ladder, keep achieving, but you know what, I do not want to!

I did not make that ladder; it is someone else's. They made it; they created it; and they hold the power as to who gets to the top or not. I want to wield my own power; I want to step off someone else's ladder and just be free.

My business is three and a half years old. I have built it from scratch. I have taught myself so much to be able to get it to a stage where I am being recognised on such levels as the Great British Entrepreneur Awards, The Family Business of the Year Awards and much more.

But what will it mean to have truly made it? When will

enough be enough? When will I stop? For me, honestly, never, as it just is not in my nature. I have taken all that ambition and drive I had when working for someone else and put it into my business. I am my own boss; I write my own hours; I make up my own rules. Knowing that if my daughter asks, "Can we go for a walk in the woods today?" I do not have to even think about it; I will not need to worry about what I will be compromising in order to take that time out of my day for her. I will not need to worry about being too tired, although I am sure mum-tired never really goes away.

I think that is when I will have truly made it. When I can start saying yes, saying yes to opportunities, saying yes to friends and family and saying yes to life.

Taking a little step back to assess and think about what this means to me gives me even more fire in my belly to achieve it. Am I there yet, hell no. Do I have financial stability, also, hell no! But is it worth it, hell f***ing yes it is!

I want to thank all the inspirational women I am surrounded by who are my cheerleaders. Hearing their stories, hearing their setbacks and how they overcame them gives me so much motivation, I watch and learn in awe.

I hope one day I can inspire, even just one person, to live their dream like others have inspired me to live mine, and then maybe, just maybe, I will have made it.

BIO

Erin Parnell is an entrepreneur and businesswoman; her business Eternally Cherished UK Ltd (www.eternallycherished.co.uk) has been featured in Vogue, Tatler, Closer, and London Life, as well as multiple features on That's TV Hampshire. Her business is multi-award winning and has been a finalist in many more awards. She crafts cherished items into stunning pieces of jewellery for people to treasure forever.

Eternally Cherished UK Ltd – www.eternallycherished.co.uk

24

FROM CORPORATE TO CREATIVE

Steph Briggs

L ike most entrepreneurs, I've had various jobs, in different industries, in entirely different roles until I discovered my true calling as an Interior Designer & Co-Founder of La Di Da Interiors, a gifts and interiors emporium. Not many people know that I am a Silversmith and Jeweller by trade. I was fortunate to gain a place at the famous Birmingham School Of Jewellery to study for my degree. However, the realities of working in the trade post-graduation left me feeling undervalued. I kept wondering why I had spent so much time studying when my creativity wasn't even enough to pay the bills!

From there, I worked in a recruitment company as an administrator and was told I didn't have 'any sales experience' so couldn't get promoted to be a consultant. I tried multi-level marketing, worked as a mystery shopper, I even sold lorries and then upgraded to sports cars (far sexier!). I became a Marketing Manager, worked as a sales rep for an equestrian herbal supplement company (and got fired!). I even ended up working for one of the most old fashioned, male-dominated law companies in the UK that ironically had assisted my previous boss in sacking me. Driving over a thousand miles per week, working ridiculously long hours in high-pressure culture with a £1m per quarter revenue target was taking its toll.

My eureka moment was winning "Salesperson of the Quarter", having worked 100 hours a week for most of the quarter, going to the sales conference (unpaid on a Saturday, of course, because you can't have any time off the road). The managing director awarded me a naff certificate printed on A4 office paper and a warm bottle of Moet and whispered in my ear, "clocks back to zero now, let's hope you can do it again this quarter".

In that second, something clicked. Yes, I was earning over £100k per year, but this guy owned me. Literally. It was a toxic culture, and I knew I wanted more. Needed more and had to escape in order;

- To remain married to the person I love.
- Regain my physical and mental health.
- Enjoy life again.
- To reignite my creative flair that had lain dormant for so long.

I had no idea what I would do, but I survived for six months in that job, trying to figure out what my next move was going to be.

What I worked out in those six months was...

- I love negotiating a deal, people like me, and I enjoy helping others – I needed to do something that involved all of these elements.
- I am a creative at heart. I love making things look

good. Being a military wife, we moved house a lot. We'd end up in Quarters with random carpets and horrendous patterned curtains. I used to paint furniture to try and give some feeling of cohesion and home wherever we ended up, even if we knew that we would be moving within the year. I found painting to be really calming and mindful.

- Every day I met with small business owners and Directors, usually helping them when they had an issue with staff, and I realised that they're all winging it to some degree! No small business owner knows everything either when they start or along the way.

- I wanted to start a family, and it was doubtful that was going to happen in the job I was in. And none of the few other women in the role I did had small children; it just wasn't compatible.

- I already had a support network around me (I just didn't see it at the time). My husband, Stu, who obviously had to deal with the grumpy, stressed person on a daily basis, was the one that said: "quit the job" and believed in me when I really didn't believe in myself. I had a network of business owners that had become friends over the years that I trusted to sound out my ideas.

- My work ethic of "if it's going to be, it's up to me" that had been drilled into me from my first sales role would see me through because if my idea didn't work, then I could always go and get another job.

What happened next

By chance (or was it?!) I saw a small Vintage and Interiors shop for sale. I went in and mystery shopped it as I would have all those years before. It was quaint and fun but dark and disor-ganised. I could immediately see so many things that I could improve quickly and easily and make it a better shopping experience. The primary item that I saw that made me think, "this is it!" was the small display of Annie Sloan Chalk Paint, identical to the one at home that I had been painting furniture with.

On 8th July 2015, I quit my job. I drove to Manchester and handed my company car, laptop and pile of contracts over. I was escorted off the premises, and I got the train back to Hampshire to start my new business.

I was excited, scared and ready to get to work.

I took a loan of £18K, and my new company vehicle was a bicycle. I bought a laptop and opened a business bank account. It all felt very surreal. After my first week, I cycled home, and Stu asked how my day had been.

"I can't believe I actually get to do this for a living", was my reply.

"I love it!"

He says that he can still remember that conversation because of the massive smile on my face that he hadn't seen for such a long, long time.

At the end of August, something happened that made me more focused than ever before. I found out that I was pregnant!

My previous project management skills came into force! This was when I realised that if I was going to have a little person in my life, there was no way that I could go back to working for anyone else. Time to plan out the next three years to get through pregnancy, become a Mummy (aged 38), and juggle life.

Year one

I focussed on learning how to run a shop/small business. I wanted evolution, not revolution. I aimed to retain the local customer base and grow a social media presence. Although I painted furniture, I knew that being a new Mummy wouldn't allow this to continue, so I became a teacher and hosted workshops. This enabled my customers to explore DIY with a guiding hand and instil faith in themselves! I found it thrilling to help people gain the confidence "to create a beautiful home", and they became long-term customers.

Our tagline was born along with our beautiful baby boy, Reuben.

Year two

Became an award-winning business for "Best Interiors Store in Hampshire" thanks to year one! I came "back to work" after maternity leave and reality bit on the cost of nursery care. I readjusted my goals and decided to "go online", and opened our website.

We were featured in our first national magazines and newspapers.

Year three

We won "Best Interiors Store in Hampshire" again. We doubled our turnover in comparison to year one. We diversified, and we won our first private interior design project – a sitting room in a barn conversion and our first commercial design and fit-out, a tasting room for Wessex Spirits. I turned 40 and started to believe in my business, although I still suffered from imposter syndrome.

First TV appearance. Stu quit his military career to join me in the business.

.

And beyond

In the following three years we have rebranded, re-designed our website and moved to larger premises. We are rated 5* by our customers for service and have a nationwide customer base. My interior design work has continued to grow with both private and commercial clients. We now turn over six times more than we did in year one. We have a thriving internet-based business as well as a showroom and have survived the pandemic. Our company has evolved, changed, diversified and adapted. I now want to create a legacy; we are now an accredited plastic-free champion, you can make your order carbon-neutral, and we are working towards being carbon negative. We have helped thousands of people to create a beautiful lifestyle.

Of course, there are some really dull bits; the VAT returns, pensions, fire risk assessments etc. BUT, being your own boss is a beautiful journey. I've learnt more about myself and grown as a person over these last six years than ever before. I'm now more confident, assertive and happy.

It's hard in a small business, particularly when you don't have many staff, to be consistently working on the business and in it. This is an area that is a work in progress for me.

Apart from the fact that I would be an even worse employee than I was before, you couldn't pay me enough to go back to employment. Not having to ask for time off to go to take and collect my little one on his first day of school is priceless and a day that I will treasure forever. My Dad had cancer and needed someone to go to the hospital with him. I was there as much as he wanted; I didn't need anyone's permission.

Find something that you're passionate about and that excites you. That will keep you going through challenging times. There will always be someone trying to copy or imitate your business. Be momentarily flattered, stay focused and annoying as it is, ignore it.

No one else is you; that is your superpower.

Look at your skillset; work to your strengths, outsource your weaknesses. I find bookkeeping and accounting incredibly dull, even though I know it's essential. I've had an accountant from day one. However, I love social media, so I do it all myself.

When I started, I wanted to run my own business to try things my own way and escape the politics and bull working for a large corporation. I wanted to serve our customers by helping them to create a beautiful retreat that they can call home. What I've learnt so far is that La Di Da Interiors is just a vehicle, yes it is my 2nd baby, but if I was to sell it tomorrow, I now have the skills, confidence and self-assurance to start a new company, to take a new direction whenever I chose to.

Steph's top tips for new entrepreneurs:

Surround yourself with a small team of people that have your back but will also be brutally honest with you – some loved ones, some paid advisers, some business peers.

Network – pass referrals and share knowledge. My Accountant, PR Guru and several of my employees have all been introduced to me through networking.

Know your numbers, get an accountant, pay the tax bill happily.

Invest in yourself; each year, I invest in a creative course and a business course or workshop. Often it's the networking and other students that are just as influential as the course content.

Get good at social media – whatever your industry.

Be prepared to pivot.

Remember, everyone is winging it!

Life is short; buy the shoes, drink the wine, eat the cake, start the business.

BIO

Steph Briggs is creative director of the award-winning independent gifts and interior retailer La Di Da Interiors and a celebrated Interior Designer. An expert in upcycling pre-loved furniture, Steph's natural talent for combining old with fabulous and new has earned her the title of 'The Queen Of Upcycling' by her contemporaries and considerable coverage on TV radio and the national press. Steph's clients include both private and commercial, and her interior design projects range from consultancy services to major renovations. As featured in *The Metro, The Daily Mirror, The Daily Express, The Daily Mail, The Lady, World of Interiors, Your Home Style, House Beautiful, The Times* and many more.

La Di Da Interiors & Gifts – www.ladida-andover.com

25

THE UNIVERSE WORKS IN MYSTERIOUS WAYS

Amanda Michaelin

The first idea I had about running my own holistic wellness business came to me around 2007. I was sat at my pokey corner desk having just finished another after-hours appointment, advising a young man that his dream of owning a home may have to wait a few years, until he could successfully fulfil the criteria required. Seeing the disappointment in his face I thought, 'This wasn't my dream'. It was already dark outside; everyone else in the agency had gone home already, but as usual, my diary, which was booked on my behalf, had a couple of late appointments, despite having to be in the office at 8:45am every day for the morning sales meeting. Exhausted, I locked away the files, locked up the office and walked to the dimly lit car park out the back, slumped into my car to drive home. At this point, I thought 'It would be so much easier being my own boss, working hours I choose, doing something that I actually enjoy'. But how would I even go about getting started?

I was no stranger to stress and burnout, having spent at that time 9 years in the corporate finance world, with some of that in management. I'd faced all its challenges: long hours, deadlines, targets and the feeling of constantly being in a pressure sandwich. And so, I enjoyed visits to the spa and massages and learning new ways to take care of myself. I'd been burned out and bounced back more times than I could remember, or so I thought.

I started dreaming more and more about taking a gap year to travel and learn holistic therapies and set myself a plan to save up enough cash to embark upon it. At this point, I'd envisaged maybe being a massage therapist or learning acupuncture. I didn't know how, but all I knew was I was going!

Fast forward to winter 2008

I walked into the office differently on this morning. With a spring in my step and an excited feeling, clasping the brown paper envelope. I handed it to my regional manager. Inside was my resignation ... I was going travelling! How? Well, the previous 12 months, I had been in a relationship with somebody, and it'd had gotten quite serious. He too shared the dream of travelling and in fact was offered a placement in China as a TEFL teacher. It wasn't the destination I'd had in mind, nor the job I'd planned, but when I was invited to join him, I thought this was a great idea and after the stress of holding together a long-distance relationship, while being miserable in my job, it seemed a no-brainer. I could probably learn the holistic therapies around teaching, get to see the world, learn, grow and 'find my zen'! So, I booked my ticket, sorted my affairs and was off on a jet plane.

Goodbye corporate world, hello future!
These lines from T.S. Eliot became a bit of a mantra for me:

What we call the beginning is often the end
And to make an end is to make a beginning.
The end is where we start from. ('Little Gidding', V, ll. 1–3)

Nothing worked out quite as I had planned. Now 2011, I found myself boarding a plane back home to the UK. No job, no money, a failed relationship, no home, debt I couldn't repay, self-esteem and health … non-existent. The rug had really been ripped out from under me this time! I felt like a total failure. I weighed about 5st5lb, my body as frail and fragile as a 1000-year-old piece of lace. Emotionally and mentally, stress finally won out! The thought of having to go back to a career which contradicted every part of my being was too much. I was diagnosed as having had a nervous breakdown and was suffering severe PTSD and anxiety. What followed was the darkest period of my life!

During 18 months of arduous recovery and whispers of 'she'll never get through this!', I often wondered if this was the end of the road for me. Battling mixed thoughts and feelings daily of, 'just give up!' verses 'no, keep fighting!'. At first following the medical and psychological route with lots of medication, I later turned to various alternative and natural methods. I had what I can only describe as an awakening! T. S. Eliot was right. Forget breakdown, this was my breakthrough! And my calling! I feel now that I experienced what I did so I could help others.

If I'd left finance and become a therapist back in 2007, I may have done okay, but now I'd learnt a natural way to live and heal, developed my intuitive gifts and overcome many layers

COMPILED BY TRUDY SIMMONS

and lifetimes of trauma. Now I was ready. I could empathise; and instead of just reading a book or a manual, I had experience. I was transformed. I also had a reason. I had an unwavering feeling that I never wanted anyone to experience what I had and knew that if I shared what I'd learnt, I could help people. The universe does work in mysterious ways.

I returned to my old occupation while I spent a few years mastering my crafts. And as a now more balanced and healed individual, I had all the tools to manage this easily, avoiding any burn out. I had no passion for this job though and knew it was a means to an end. When the opportunity arose to leave the finance job behind and embark on my self-employment journey, with the support and encouragement of my partner, family, and friends, I launched my healing and guidance business.

Alongside Soul Serenity Healing, I also joined a social selling company for natural skincare and cosmetics because the products were amazing: I used them myself and the ethos matched me and my beliefs perfectly. So now I was officially the owner of two businesses, and also launching Skin Serenity.

Waking up with passion, not dread

So ... what has running my own business been like? Working the hours, I choose. Tick. Doing something that I actually enjoy. Tick. Easier being my own boss? Hmm yes and no. It is amazing being able to work the hours I choose, enabling a more balanced life, ensuring I have enough time for my family, friends, hobbies, and self-care time. After all, life isn't all about work. We are human beings, not human doings. I absolutely love what I do. So much so it doesn't feel like work at all! Every day is different. Helping others blossom through their own healing transformations or seeing them action guidance with success brings me so much joy. Being my own boss means no more power suits, stuffy offices, hierarchical nonsense. I can work in the park should I so choose, or down the coffee shop. The only targets being set are ones I set myself.

Being my own boss, however, has opened up new challenges for me. While a lot of the skills I learnt in the corporate world are transferable and have been invaluable, I don't possess every skill I need. I quickly learnt that I was every role in my business. The CEO, the branding and marketing department, the accounts department, the sales and service departments, the production, packaging, and dispatch departments. And while I loved the extra time and freedom being self-employed gave me, that quickly became absorbed by all of these roles – some of which I had no clue about: e.g., the IT Department. Scheduling and time blocking became my new best friend. It is a real art juggling so many plates.

The other challenge that presented itself was being a small business: I didn't start out with oodles of investment to plough in, making it difficult to outsource any of the roles. It has been a steep learning curve. The biggest difference came when I found networking community groups like Hampshire Women's Business Group. These enabled me to meet and speak to other women in similar positions, either looking for help with a different department of their business or being able to offer me their services. These spaces have become an integral part of my schedule. A place where we all support each other, inspire each other, and celebrate each other's successes. We are not alone. In some cases, I have had to further my study and learn new skills, but this has only helped grow my confidence and commitment to my business.

Facing new challenges

I have thus far run my business face-to-face and via referrals, so the recent pandemic posed some challenges. I do have social media accounts but have utilised them only sporadically. I very quickly had to learn to take things online. As mentioned earlier, IT was not a skill I possessed. After the initial 'What does this button do?' and the 'Can you hear me? Can you see me?' conversations, I'm navigating several platforms with a measure of skill and have successfully moved some services online.

I'm currently extending my newfound IT skills to develop my shiny new website, with the assistance of one of the businesses I met through networking. My plan is to get everything online in the very near future, so watch this space. It is the Age of Aquarius now, so technology is the future and I have to move with the times. Being adaptable is a skill every business owner needs.

I do have a vision for the future of my business and will keep working towards it, day by day. Goals being set, the timescale is fluid, and it may change. Part of that vision is to continue learning and growing in skill and mastery. Sharing what I learn so that others too can feel healthier, more empowered, and live a more balanced and serene existence.

When thinking about where I am right now on my business journey and what the future holds for Soul Serenity Healing and Guidance, I ask myself these questions: is it all worth it? And the answer is an easy yes. What is success to me? To me, success is like beauty, it's in the eye of the beholder. Am I successful? Well, I feel like I'm winning every day. I'm incredibly happy and to me that is what everything is all about, it's why we are here, to live a joyous life. Of course, life has its ups and downs. Business owning has its challenges and its celebrations, but ultimately, we grow through adversities and come out stronger. If I can help just one person, if one word I say inspires someone, saves someone, transforms someone's life, then that is success!

If you can take one thing from my story, let it be that health is wealth and if you are sat there right now with a dream to own your own business, or any kind of goal or dream, put it out to the universe, you may be surprised: it does work in mysterious ways.

And if you are already a business owner and/or are struggling with stress, challenges or feeling like you're failing, I leave you with two further quotes (I do love a quote!) that made an impact on me, in my journey. And I wish you all the very best.

'It's always darkest before the dawn' – Thomas Fuller

'Many of life's failures are people who did not realise how close they were to success' – Thomas A. Edison

BIO

Amanda Michaelin is a Reiki Master Teacher, Multidimensional Healer, Intuitive Reader, Astrologer and Spiritual Teacher at Soul Serenity Healing and Guidance.

She uses her wealth of experience and training to guide, support, and facilitate healing for people who are experiencing challenges on their journey through life. Providing a safe space for transformation and the rebalance of the mind, body and soul to its natural serenity. Amanda also teaches spiritual development.

Soul Serenity Healing and Guidance – www.soulserenityhg.com

26

THE GREAT S-CAPE

Claudia Beard

Superhero capes for children. A simple concept right? But why "I Am Super Capes" exactly?

I started I Am Super Capes in 2014, with one mantra in mind: that every child deserves to be a hero, no matter their story. Putting a handmade superhero cape on, one made with love, with thought and with respect, makes any Little Hero feel as special as they deserve to feel.

I am a single mother of three boys. These boys are my world, every single thing I do, every action, every decision is thought out to make sure they know they are loved, seen and valued. However, there are a lot of children out there that don't feel that. They don't feel like the Little Hero that they are; this is what I wanted to change. I wanted to give children the POWER to be children, despite any illness, disability, or social standing – for them to just feel special.

I know first-hand what it is like to have a Little Hero. My

youngest has a host of complex needs, and I know what it's like for these children to be thrust into an adult medical world. Many tests, appointments, therapies, and medicine. There is sometimes no time to just be a child, to play, to imagine. When your days are spent in hospital or in a doctor's office or with a therapist, there is little time to just play. For the child to just be a child. That is why I wanted something that they can take with them, something to remind them they are HEROES; they deserve to feel special, to feel strong and brave and most importantly, to be a child.

Would anyone else love my idea?

In December 2014 I sent out a few social media posts about what I was planning. I loved the idea of Super Capes, but I wasn't sure anyone else would. Keeping the social media posts simple, I just said I wanted to reuse children's duvet covers and turn them into Superhero Capes to send to children in hospital, children fighting an illness, children with disabilities or children's charities.

I was blown away by the response. It completely snowballed. So many people wanted to be involved. The feedback I got was so full of love and encouragement and so many messages asking 'how can I be involved'. I was at a total loss for words and so humbled that this simple idea was met with so much love and encouragement.

I have sent over 800 Superhero Capes out into the world. There are 800 Little Heroes with a cape made by I Am Super Capes making them feel stronger. The stories started coming in from parents/carers of these Little Heroes. Stories like how a Little Hero would take his cape with him when he went for his chemo treatment, as it made him feel stronger. Stories like a Little Hero who wore his cape right up until he went into theatre to have his leg amputated due to a horrendous infection.

Stories like a room full of Little Heroes having a day out from being young carers themselves and getting to decorate and design their own cape and then leave with their own creation. A chance for them to be children. We gave them the power to just be children.

I wanted to create the charity in two ways. Capes for Little Heroes and Super Missions. The capes for our Little Heroes would come via nominations. I would get emails from family members, friends, even medical staff who know the Little Hero. They would email me all about them, about their life, their strengths, their hobbies and what cartoon character/superhero character they liked most, as well as their favourite colours and I would source the fabric, or purchase it myself, to personalise the Super Cape.

Our Super Missions worked slightly differently, as we needed quite a few capes for one mission. Again I would get an email from a charity or organisation that worked with children. I would then use bright, happy fabric, mostly children's duvets (which are perfect for capes), wrap them up and courier them out to the charity or organisation.

One of my favourite missions was working with Winchester Young Carers. An organisation that is very close to my heart. Instead of taking completed capes in, I decided to let these amazing Heroes decorate their own capes. So I made up plain white capes and took in loads of scrap fabrics, fabric pens, etc. The final results were brilliant. To see the creativity, the thought processes, and the finished capes was great, but best of all was to see the pride in each of those children's faces, to see them running around wearing their own cape, to see them feeling like Superheroes, well there are no words.

Our capes have been sent to the Philippines, Portugal, Ireland, and right here in the UK. I also had the fantastic opportunity to take 450 capes to the Red Cross Children's Hospital in Cape Town, South Africa. I got to personally walk around with the amazing nurses, doctors, and volunteers who run the hospital and meet some families and hear their stories. But best of all I got to meet so many Little Heroes, to hold their hands, play with them if I could and give them their capes.

What I also love about I Am Super Capes is the community it has grown. Not only among all our Little Heroes, their families and friends but the amazing Super Sewers who would get together every so often and spend a full day cutting, trimming, sewing and ironing as many capes as possible. We even have some Mini Super Sewers joining us. Kids sewing capes for kids, could there be anything better?

New skills, new business

But did you know that when I started I Am Super Capes...I didn't know how to sew? It sounds ludicrous, I know, but I had a vision, and I knew what I wanted to make. I found someone in my village who knew how to sew and took some lessons with her and learnt how to sew a superhero cape. A small achievement that I am proud of, and a lesson to myself that when you have a vision, you just have to find a way of getting it done.

In May 2020 I took this newfound skill and decided to turn it into a business. In the middle of a global pandemic, not the best time I know, but I love a challenge.

As a newly single mother of three boys, I was starting from scratch. I needed to bring in some income, and I needed to do it around my boys being home as all the schools were closed and they were home schooling.

And so, Starry Llama was born. And it was born on the cusp of face masks being made mandatory. While face masks weren't going to be a core product, I received a request to make a face mask (I had never made one before), but after a lot of trial and error I learnt to make them.

Then I got an order for another and another and within

seven months I had handmade over 1700 masks. A fantastic achievement, and one that still makes me feel proud.

These orders were getting my business known. The excitement every time I got an order was immense. The pride I felt every time I sent an order out was immense. I did this; I created this business from nothing and on the back of becoming a single mother. I created this business in the midst of a global pandemic. I created this business with three children at home because their schools were closed. I created this business when I didn't think I could create something like Starry Llama.

Juggling on a rollercoaster

Running a business, for me, is like riding on a rollercoaster while juggling a lot of balls in the air. It is exciting, exhilarating, exhausting, difficult, and emotional. The highs are amazing, the lows are terrifying, but it is definitely a ride worth taking. I have learnt so much and I continue to learn. I have also made so many mistakes – something I found is necessary in business. I have learnt not to be afraid of the mistakes and the failures. I have also learnt not to take them too personally, but instead to analyse, learn, put something in place to avoid it happening again, and to move on.

I am still on the rollercoaster, and I am having the time of my life!

Claudia Beard is the founder of I Am Super Capes, a charity making Superhero Capes for children in hospital, children fighting and illness and children's charities, and Starry Llama, a business making quality handmade products using bright and vibrant fabric.

BIO

Claudia lives with her three amazing boys: Broden (15), Chase (9) and Trent (8). They all live in a village outside of Winchester. As well as running her charity and business, Claudia is a full-time carer to her youngest son who has complex additional needs.

I Am Super capes & Starry Llama – www.iamsupercapes.co.uk

UNWAVERING BELIEF

Belinda Jane Sampson

My very first bricks and mortar premise was actually wood and glue as it was a simple shed in a garden centre. Let me take you back to how I started.

I've always felt that there needs to be 'people places', places that we can all use to just be; be together, be creative, time out and feel better on leaving, than when we arrived. I visualised and have built a business that offers creativity, space for being together and the sale of supplies. My golden goal is to be the Largest Craft Business in the South East of England!

My very first beginnings after leaving university was charity work. Particularly fundraising and marketing which I absolutely loved. I certainly felt like I made a difference to the lives we supported. It impressed me that the two charities I worked for could have a need, fundraise for that need and solve a problem. I wanted to be able to do that. I wanted to be able to write a cheque (yes, I'm old school!) and hand it to someone or a group that I could make an immediate difference to. This was just one of the reasons why I wanted to establish BellaCrafts.

I am also very passionate about people. I am one of six children, second eldest and have always lived in a very busy, happy and hardworking family. For ten years there were the five of us, my mum and her first four children. And as you can imagine, it was hard as a single mother with four children all under the age of six years with dad leaving. I think this is what instilled in me, my fierce determination and hardworking ethic. Of course, with my background comes a lot of feelings of also proving one's self which you have to manage! It is a huge driving force but you have to make sure you also realise your achievements.

So, back to the shed! During my years of fundraising as a side line I began to make jewellery. I first became hooked after attending a silversmith course. And with this new hobby I was keen to make this into a money-making side line. I remember Christmas 2006 I sold 25 bracelets and a number of handmade cards…. I was in the money! Ha! I had a lot to learn about the true expenses of a business.

Then shortly after, during one of my fundraising meetings and having some of my jewellery admired and of course me explaining I would love a shop… I was offered a shed, literally three by three metres to rent in the grounds of that local garden centre. I clearly grabbed with both hand, although it was very cold, leaked and the rent, for what it was, was very high!

I opened my shed on the 1st December 2007 and it was so small I had to step outside when more than three people popped in! Me, being me, I knew my ambition was more and I needed much more room! So, on the 23rd December I asked the garden centre for a piece of land to rent and upon which I built a larger, pretty cabin. The cabin was filled with craft supplies to buy, we ran workshops, parties and offered a welcoming space to women by themselves, families, friends, business, communities; everyone.

At this stage I was still working full time in my charity role so in April 2008 I took on my first member of staff. Another huge learning curve over the many years and often unexpected experiences.

I loved it. We had started in the small shed, some days taking just £3 but with our now larger cabin we started to see more customers and more bookings. Of course, we soon outgrew this space as well, so in May 2009 we moved into our beautiful barn in Fair Oak Garden Centre, Hampshire where we still have one of our centres. I have always felt very lucky in securing this first bricks and mortar premise as I had to give a presentation and promise I was a successful business (with obviously the only track record of residing in sheds!). Luckily, the decision maker was a man who advocated small business and had run several himself so he either thought I'd make a success of it or felt sorry for me! The other very important plan I had to make was to make sure I could afford it! I created my first business plan, with all the expenses and hopefully incomings to cover the first six months. I could then offer notice to leave if I needed to. I decided that even if everything went wrong, I would have to borrow monies and pay everything back, no doubt over a long time! My parents very kindly paid the deposit of about £1300 and surprisingly, I have never looked back! And nor did I borrow any further funds until we expanded in 2019. I grew the business steadily and organically. Perhaps, not the easiest way and certainly took longer but this was just after the banking crash of 2007 so no one was going to lend a young, fresh, female in a new business any cash!

We grew our offerings, our craft ranges, learnt about wholesale and I even visited the massive Chinese's trade fairs! I kept pushing our parties, offered our space, created new workshops and continued to attend local events to get our name out there.

Now, you might be wondering about the name; BellaCrafts. It took a while to decide and I still have my notebook I used to create this name. Lists and lists of words, joining together and looking into meanings. I settled on Bella, meaning beautiful in Italian and of course Crafts as it says what it does on the tin! Little did I know that later this would pay dividends with social media!

Nowadays Bella is a popular name so it is mistaken that the business is named after me. It's not as I am quite happy blending into the team! My team are always just as good as me, often better at their roles and I immensely enjoy working with and learning from them.

In 2010 I made a decision. One I know a lot of business owners struggle with, giving up the day job! I had worked within the charity sector for many years and had reached management levels but the way I made the decision to leave and dedicate myself fully to BellaCrafts was, I thought I could always return to a job but not always have the opportunity to take a leap and give my absolute all to my business. Something I am yet to regret!

Around 2014 my younger sister was unsure what she wanted to do after finishing college. She had some very impressive exam results and had certainly applied herself over the years. She had hit burnout so wanted to take a year out and try a new working environment. This was one of my proudest moments having my sister join me, in what now had become 'a proper business'. We immensely enjoy working together and she's still in the business today and it is one of my favourite things to have happened. Of course, she may move on and anyone would be lucky to have her! But for now, I feel we're a formidable pair enjoying the benefits of growing the business and being able to implement so many new ideas and revenue streams. We are both very creative, practical and thankfully my sister has a wise head to rein in my wacky ideas!

We always work for all the team and just as it is important to provide our customers with an amazing experience, we believe that our team is one of our most important assets. We work on offering competitive rates of pay, a very supportive environment where training and learning is encouraged and many tangible benefits. If your team is happy, your whole place is happy.

Having built the business over several years we then felt we needed to complement our Centre at Fair Oak. It was, and still is, an exciting time for BellaCrafts and in 2019 we approached landlords to ask if they had any suitable premises to open a second Centre. Winchester Council happened to have the perfect space! In October 2019 we opened our Craft House and Tea Rooms in Kings Walk, Winchester with two floors, tea rooms and soft play and of course with space for people, groups, families and business. We will always keep our ethos of offering space every day for people to use individually and in groups to be together.

There is such a need, not least since we have all just experienced one of the most challenging times with the effects of Covid-19, of us all valuing the importance of people. 'People make life worth living', my mother has always impressed upon me and she's right!

As Covid hit in March 2020 our businesses were shut down overnight with not much of a contingency. It has been a tough time! It has been a time of worry not least for the business but our families, friends and team.

But us being us, we bounced back! We learnt how to Zoom and virtually support our team, we learnt how to develop our workshops online, we built our online shop of crafty supplies, we developed new craft products such as our MakeMe Craft & Gift ranges, and our new adult and children's craft subscription boxes. We also purchased a laser cutter to make our own kits and personalised products. We increased our advertising, offerings on social media including a YouTube channel full of crafty projects and offered many free ideas to help keep a nation entertained. We created a whole new virtual business which is here to stay!

We've now re-opened our centres again, and are fighting back and we are definitely winning against this dreadful virus. Slowly and surely.

On a personal note, I also had my second child, my adorable baby boy in April 2020 which brought its own challenges! He added to my very supportive, amazing husband, Daniel and my other beautiful son Harrison.

I have always had a very laser focused goal of what I want my business to offer and where I want my business to reach. I have had to hold unwavering belief in my goals, take calculated risks and keep believing in people and myself. To starting Bella-Crafts from just selling handmade jewellery to my aim of reaching my financial goal of a steady seven-figure turnover I believe hard work and surrounding yourself with great people is the key.

Here's to our exciting future. We will continue to develop our successful programme of events to businesses, communities and schools, we will grow our customer base on and offline, expand our own products to sell nationally and wholesale and decide to expand and / or franchise when the time is right.

Thank you so much to all those who have been and continue to be a part of BellaCrafts.

A business is a bit like having children: you know you love it, but just wish they both came with a better manual!

With special thanks to my family and Victoria.

BIO

Belinda Jane Sampson is the proud owner of Harrison and

Theodore Sampson, keeper of Daniel Sampson and proud member of my massive, fantastic family.

BellaCrafts is an Award-winning Craft & Activity Centre
For children, adults, business, family and community
Parties, events, workshops, festivals and craft supplies.

BellaCrafts Ltd – www.bellacrafts.co.uk

FINALLY GETTING ALL OF WHAT I WANT

Jennifer Jones

W hen I was about 8 years old, my music teacher was Dr Robert Lee Kidd III, or Bob, as he was known to all of his students. That's when I figured out you could be a doctor of something other than medicine and decided I wanted to get a PhD.

When I started uni, at the University of Oklahoma, I thought I'd be a music teacher. That changed when we were asked to think about how we'd really respond to being the only teacher in a room full of kids with instruments they didn't know how to play – I realised that I would have left and locked the door behind me. I changed my music education course for a musical arts course and carried on.

My new course required that I take several modules across the arts and humanities, and I loved exploring ideas: art history, British history, and English literature – I could have stayed forever. Since I couldn't afford to be a perpetual student, I had to start thinking about what I wanted to do.

I've always been drawn to teaching. When we were kids, every summer I'd take my younger sister and cousin to the library and help them choose a topic to study for the summer. We'd find books, and I'd help them develop reports and presentations – looking back, I'm shocked they were so cooperative. Books and writing were my thing, not theirs.

I briefly toyed with becoming a teacher, but I didn't love the idea of dealing with a room full of kids, even without instruments in hand. So I decided to get a PhD and become a lecturer. I added a BA in English to my musical arts degree and went off to the University of California at Davis for my PhD.

I loved the studying and teaching I did there, but it wasn't all smooth sailing.

Love, happiness, and profound uncertainty

In 2005 my life was turned upside down. In March, I adopted Maggie, my cat (she's now about 20 years old and napping in the next room). In August, I met Chris and we started a long-distance (California, USA to Exeter, UK) relationship. In October, I was diagnosed with my first autoimmune condition: Hashimoto's thyroiditis.

In 2006 Chris and I got engaged and I was diagnosed with relapsing remitting multiple sclerosis. In 2007 we got married and I moved to the UK. In 2008, I finished my PhD.

Laid out in two short paragraphs, all that upheaval looks manageable. It wasn't. Just as I was getting my head around my new health reality and learning how to manage my energy levels, I was embarking on years of gruelling job searches and precarious (and exploitative) employment.

Over the next 8 years, I'd work with hundreds of students as a part-time lecturer, and I loved sharing my research with them and watching them develop intellectually. I didn't love the rigid systems, endless admin, and hours of unpaid work.

For a while, I bought the lie that I had to pay my dues and believed it would eventually pay off and I'd get a full-time post. By 2016, it was clear that wasn't going to happen, and even if it did, I wouldn't get a post close enough to where Chris taught for us to live together. I didn't get married and move across the Atlantic to still not live with him. Also, I was mentally and physically exhausted. Clearly, something had to change, so I left.

Life beyond the university

Leaving academia was one of the hardest things I've ever done. It was only upon leaving that I realised how much of my identity was wrapped up in being an academic. How was I supposed to figure out what I wanted to do when I didn't even know who I was anymore?

Unpicking that tangled mess is an ongoing process. I'm not sure it will ever be finished and now see myself as a recovering academic; yes, just as people in 12-step programmes are always recovering, not recovered.

At times, the process has been excruciatingly painful, like the first few times I had to attend events on campus; my husband is still an academic, as are many of our friends – I couldn't avoid it forever. I had to dig deep to find the strength to smile politely when I wanted to scream and cry. Going out with our academic friends could be trying. They often talked shop and for years I'd joined in because I was teaching in the same department as them. Now, I was an outsider having to listen to them moan (for entirely justifiable reasons) about the life I desperately wanted.

Putting a brave face on things was exhausting. Still, the drive and determination that saw me through my degrees and years as a lecturer kept me from wallowing in the grief forever. By 2017, I'd completed training in proofreading and editing in British English and set up as an editor. I'd been taking on freelance editing work since 2001, so it seemed a sensible choice.

Over the next couple of years, I learnt two important things: I liked being self-employed and I really missed teaching. I was also surprised by how much writing I had to do for my business: blog posts, newsletters, social media posts – it was never ending.

I'd trained to teach writing during my PhD and had several publications to my name before I started my business, so I realised if I was finding all the writing a bit much, business owners with less writing experience likely needed a little help.

I (very) briefly toyed with the idea of becoming a copywriter, but that had a few strikes against it. I'm not gifted at embodying someone else's voice on the page. I hate being told what to write. And I'd still be doing text-based work, not teaching.

Algorithm to the rescue

Amongst businessowners, social media algorithms get a lot of stick, but the Facebook algorithm helped me figure out how to use my skills to do what I actually wanted to do. In its infinite wisdom, the algorithm thought I needed to see lots of ads from writing coaches.

Until then, I hadn't realised there was such a thing as a writing coach. Academia's a fairly insular place, and I've only recently seen academics start engaging with coaching. This was a new and exciting world!

As I was thinking about how I could go about setting myself up as a writing coach, I came across an event in Fareham on MeetUp with the Hampshire Women's Business Group. The host, Trudy Simmons, looked nice and friendly, so after checking that Fareham was only a short train ride away and the venue was in walking distance to the station, I signed up.

I'd never been to a networking meeting before and had no idea what to expect. I was greeted with a warm welcome;

everyone I met that morning was lovely and supportive. I had found my people: women businessowners.

The next chapter

A lot has happened since that morning in Fareham in 2018. I've written and published a book, There's a Book in Every Expert (that's you!): How to write your credibility-building book in six months (2020); created a six-month coaching programme based on the book; and celebrated publication days with clients for their books. In the last few months, I've trained for and launched my speaking career and have started being booked for international stages like the 2021 Women|Future Conference.

If you had told 8-year-old me that one day I'd be seeking out opportunities to speak in front of large groups of people, I'd have questioned your sanity. Back then I was too shy even to answer questions in class, as would be the case until well into my twenties. If you had told me in 2016 that in just a few short years I wouldn't feel like a crushed wreck of my former self, and instead, I'd be a confident businessowner well on her way to building a business she was proud of, I'd have thought you were just being cruel or wasting my time.

Building my business, Entrepreneurs' Writing Club, has not been easy, but I wouldn't trade it for anything. I've created a business that gives me everything I loved about academia: watching the writers I work with grow in confidence, having time to write and publish my own work, and sharing my work with others from the stage. What's more, I now don't have to deal with any of the things I came to loathe about academia.

A couple of years ago, my dad asked which was harder: getting the PhD or building my business. By far, building my business has been harder. The PhD came with a supervisor to show me the way. The business, especially before I found my people, has been mostly me trying to figure out what I want to do, how to do it all, and how to sort through the noise on the internet.

The pandemic has compounded some of the difficulties, but also brought us interesting new ways of working. Being forced to take everything online since early 2020 has shown a lot of us that we don't need to travel as much as we did before. Networking groups are keeping online meetings, even as some of them start meeting face-to-face on occasion, because busy businessowners have come to appreciate not having to schedule time to travel to and from each meeting.

Over the last year, I've learnt how to work with these changes. Since learning that just because I now can attend a (virtual) meeting doesn't mean I have to; many of the changes have been better for managing my energy levels and my business. I now meet and work with people across the world without wearing myself out with travel. Before the pandemic, going to a networking meeting that was just a short train ride away meant giving up several hours and most of my energy for that day. Now, going to a meeting on another continent means opening a Zoom call.

The time and energy that I save with this new way of working have contributed to the changes I'm seeing in my business. It's given me more space to figure out where I want my business to go and how I'm going to get there. As my business grows and changes, I'm sure there will be new challenges, but I'm looking forward to whatever the future brings.

BIO

Published author and expert writing coach, Dr Jennifer Jones has been helping people become happier, more productive writers since 2001. She trained to teach writing during her PhD at the University of California at Davis. She has taught at universities in the US and the UK, and now coaches consultants, coaches, and healers to write their credibility-building books. Jennifer's book, There's a Book in Every Expert (that's you!), came out to rave reviews in 2020. When she's not talking about writing, she can often be found researching and writing about Victorian anaesthesia, medicine, and popular culture.

Dr Jennifer Jones - Writing Coach – www.ewc.coach

ABOUT THE DAISY CHAIN GROUP

Trudy Simmons started The Daisy Chain Group in 2010. It was started to support and encourage businesswomen to have a safe space to share their journeys, and to be seen and heard in their endeavours.

Since its inception, the concept has grown to include platforms for women to find their voice and become more visible in lots of different ways. Whether it is attending The Crazy Daisy Networking events to grow your audience, coming along to The Spectacular Online Business Symposium to learn from world class speakers from around the globe, Make the opportunity to speak at The Spectacular to share your wisdom, be a part of the Shine On You Crazy Daisy book series to share your story, or be on the Shine On You Crazy Daisy Podcast to give your story gravitas and hear it in your own voice.

The Daisy Chain Group also offers The Accountability Club for businesswomen to work out how to build momentum and consistency in their businesses by deciding where their challenges are, how to overcome them and what they are committing to for the next 2 weeks - this is GOLD if you are a procrastinator (I see you!), or if you want to grow your business.

The Accountability Club is direct help and support from Trudy with her no BS way of cutting through the challenges and being able to find the next action steps to help you to move forward.

Trudy is known for her engaged communities on Facebook - The Hampshire Women's Business Group (for local businesswomen) and The International Women's Business Group (for any businesswoman that wants or has a global audience).

HAVING FUN in your business is a core value of The Daisy Chain Group. Having fun and TAKING ACTION is what builds you AND your business.

You can find The Daisy Chain Group here:
www.thedaisychaingroup.com
https://www.facebook.com/daisychaingroup
https://www.instagram.com/daisychaingroup/
https://www.linkedin.com/in/trudysimmons/

You can find The Daisy Chain Group communities here:
https://www.facebook.com/groups/hampshirewomensbusiness
https://www.facebook.com/groups/internationalwomensbusiness

You can find our services here:
The Crazy Daisy Networking - www.thedaisychaingroup.com/crazy-daisy-networking-club
The Accountability Club - www.thedaisychaingroup.com/the-accountability-club

You can find the Shine On You Crazy Daisy Podcast here:
https://www.thedaisychaingroup.com/podcasts/shine-on-you-crazy-daisy

EVERY TIME YOU BUY FROM A SMALL
BUSINESS, THEY DO A HAPPY
DANCE!

As we gain, so can we give.

10% of the profits from this book will be donated to Healthcare
Workers' Foundation Family Fund. The fund will support the
children and families of healthcare workers who have passed
due to Covid-19. To donate or support this incredible charity,
please go to this link - https://gofund.me/8aed0fc3

COMING SOON

Shine On You Crazy Daisy
Volume 2

Available from October 2021 - more stories, more inspiration, more motivation to get out there and do what you want to do with your business. We are all in this together.

.

SHINE ON YOU CRAZY DAISY
MEMBERSHIP

Do you want to be a part of something that will help you to SHINE BRIGHT in your business?

This membership will give you the opportunity to gain knowledge and the momentum to implement growth in your business.

For just £27 per month (incl. VAT), you will receive:

An actionable workshop from an expert in their field per month.

A "Crazy Daisy Working Day" – what is this you ask? Well... brace yourselves! It is an online version of co-working, we will sit together and GET STUFF DONE to work ON our business and not just in it! And I will be there to offer support and help if you need it!

And all of this for just £27 per month!

Go to this link to find out more and build your business, so that it SHINES!

www.thedaisychaingroup.com/shine-on-you-crazy-daisy-membership